Harry Howard

Hong Kong, 1997

HARRY HOWARD

*Memoirs of an Expat, Frequent-Flyer,
Cross-Culture Golden Retriever*

with **JULIE HOWARD**

FOURTH PRINTING: 2014

14 15 16 17 18 5 4 3 2 1

J Mac Publications

Printed and bound in Thailand by Pattrara Prepress

Cataloguing data available from Library and Archives Canada
ISBN 978-0-99211-92-0-1 (pbk.)
ISBN 978-0-9921192-1-8 (ebook)

Editing by Shirarose Wilensky
Cover and interior design by Gerilee McBride
Cover illustration by Marta Nielsen
Photographs courtesy of the author
Watercolor of Harry on page 65 by François Darov
Painting of woman poling down the river on page 108 by Thuy

CONTENTS

PREFACE

Anyone who travels in Asia becomes instantly aware of how easily sensory experiences lend themselves to expression, whether through photography, writing or art. I spent my early days in Tokyo wandering the maze of back streets that are the gateway to the local life of millions of seemingly urbane city dwellers who in reality are hardworking residents of hundreds of individual and unique villages within this giant metropolis. What struck me first during those dog days of summer were the smells. Mine had been confined to the purities of Canadian air, the saltiness of the sea and the freshness of cut cedar after a hard rain. These were the hot, humid smells of an Asian summer mingled with aromas exuding from the kitchens of Tokyo. Along with them came the vibrant color, the constant motion and an infinite number of contrasts that seemed to jump out at me every time I turned around.

I began writing for the love of it almost immediately. Often I would produce bits and pieces to send home to family and friends to try to give them a sense of our new environment and the changes in our lives. At one stage, an illustrated seasonal cookbook became a vehicle for writing about Japan; other thoughts and memories of China, Thailand and Vietnam, or accounts of treks through Nepal and Bhutan, were recorded in my journals.

As time went on and we moved from country to country, I wanted to write more, because this was our life—a life full of rich and diverse experiences that I thought deserved to be shared—but somehow, the challenge seemed overwhelming. I didn't know where to begin or how to tie it all together, until one morning in Saigon, following profuse apologies to the bread lady after Harry, our Golden Retriever, had snatched a baguette from the back of her bicycle, a light suddenly went on.

Soon after, Harry began writing the memoirs of his life and his humans' lives as *người nước ngoài* (translated "humans living outside their country"). Although the book is written through Harry's eyes, his stories are ours as well, based on actual events during the course of his lifetime in Asia. My objective was for Harry to take readers on a journey through the wild, untamed parts of Hong Kong and the other cities and countries he lived in to let them see the impacts of change and the effects of a curious affliction his humans often struggled with known as culture shock, to share some of the most joyful moments of his life and to look at his own reactions and emotions during life-changing events, such as the arrival of his sisters, Brie and Mali; the loss of Brie in Saigon; and, ultimately, his own death.

Throughout the book, I tried to put myself in Harry's shoes (so to speak) so that his tales would convey to readers how he felt at the time. In order to do this, I had to give him the wherewithal and wisdom to describe and reflect on life as he saw it, reminding myself at the same time that although he was a very wise soul with an innate intelligence, at the end of the day, he was still a dog.

I am convinced that if you have ever left your own familiar environment where you were able to function easily and successfully and suddenly found yourself disconnected and vulnerable as "a stranger in a strange land," you will be able to relate to Harry's tales in a heartbeat. For those who prefer to travel vicariously, my hope is that a story told by a dog as worldly as Harry will not only captivate your interest but stir your emotions. Who knows? You may even decide to venture into terra incognita.

ACKNOWLEDGMENTS

I am immensely grateful for the opportunities that have enabled Michael and me to take this extraordinary journey through Asia—a journey that Harry was part of for most of his life. We have been fortunate to have experienced the incredible diversity of the region by living in a number of different countries, and although it would invariably hit us on arrival that we were completely unfamiliar with almost everything, unable to communicate or perform even the simplest everyday tasks and at risk of an untimely end just attempting to cross the street, it has been an amazing adventure and one we wouldn't have missed for the world.

I have Harry to thank for being unable to resist the temptation to "borrow" a nice warm baguette from the bread lady's basket that morning in Saigon, causing the light to go on and providing the incentive for him to begin writing his memoirs. Additional thanks go to all three of our dogs for being part of a wonderful breed that takes a fairly laid back approach to life, is seldom undone by anything and generally goes with the flow—essential qualities for survival as an expat in Asia.

Shirarose Wilensky, my editor from Vancouver, had a sense of Harry from the beginning. Her intelligence, insight, gift of the language, astute comments and sound advice, along with a very discerning eye that picked up inconsistencies and cross-checked everything, brought the book to fruition. She kept this first-time writer on track, gently and patiently, encouraging me throughout the process and showing genuine excitement as we came closer to completion. I cannot credit her enough. I had a lovely image of her in my mind from the soft demeanor she conveyed in her emails, and when I met her for the first time in Vancouver, after the edit had been completed, she was exactly as I pictured her. Thank you, Shirarose.

The cover and interior designer, Gerilee McBride, is of the same caliber. She has created a dynamic cover from a painting by an artist I met in Vietnam that reflects Harry's personality perfectly, as well as the color of chaos. She has converted photographs to black and white and demonstrated her skill as a graphic designer in presenting an artistic and beautifully finished product. Thanks to Michael Pomije as well, for his invaluable guidance through this ever-changing world of publishing.

Friends and family have put up with me talking tirelessly about Harry's Memoirs. Sara, Steffi, Darrell and David, and Joe, thank you for your patience and abiding belief that this book would finally be published. Michael, for your wisdom, your constancy and your good humor. My love, as always.

To my Mickey. What an amazing ride.

CHAPTER 1
Survival in Terra Incognita

It hasn't been your ordinary walk in the park, I can tell you that right off the bat, but no one ever said it would be—except my Humans, who don't always tell it like it is, but I'll get to that later. The first thing I need to do is introduce myself.

My name is Harry and, no, I am not *the* renowned Harry from the Hogwarts School of Witchcraft and Wizardry, though I'm pretty sure I've had some encounters with his kind. For the record, I'm just plain old Harry the Dawg, enrolled in the School of Life, which may sound a little boring to you, but trust me, my life has been anything but!

I was born in Canada and have six brothers and sisters dispersed throughout the Lower Mainland near Vancouver, which is on the west coast of North America, looking out toward Japan. I was six weeks old when my Humans brought me home and had no idea it was the beginning of a lifetime of adventures that would turn me into an expat, frequent-flyer, cross-culture dawg. Call it fate, destiny, good fortune, whatever you will, but here I am, nine years later, just beginning to write my "Tails" from Ho Chi Minh City, formerly Saigon, during *mùa mưa*, having spent puppyhood in Hong Kong, puberty in Vancouver and adolescence in Hanoi and Chiangmai. I never dreamed I'd be back in Vietnam for a second tour of duty, but here I am.

In case you're wondering about *mùa mưa,* it's rainy season, which happens every year across Asia, come hell or high water. The biggest storms arrive on the heels of hot spells, with loud rumbles and zig-zaggy lightning, and require a hasty retreat under your Mom's computer at the sound of the first thunderclap.

My Humans contend I'm the most well-loved breed of dawg that ever walked the face of the earth, so "plain" would hardly be the word they'd use to describe me or my sisters, Brie and Mali. Brie wasn't my real sister—we adopted her when she was eight months old, not long before we moved to Hanoi. As for Mali, she's an amazing story all on her own that will be revealed in the fullness of time.

The PAW-LITICALLY correct name for us is Golden Retrievers, but we're often called mellow yellows, because we're gentle by nature (ergo my email address: harry@harry.calm) and equally affectionate to everyone we meet, even if they happen to be vicious intruders who have smashed the upstairs window, triggered the alarm and are about to escape with the entire contents of our house.

From the very first day I met my Humans, I knew instinctively that my mission in life was to let them know I loved them more than anything in the world and to do everything in my power to make them love me just as much. It was basically a full-time job that kept me busy from morning till night, tearing through the house looking for anything of theirs to chew on, jumping up to lick their faces whenever the opportunity presented itself and doing my utmost to remember that the newspapers strewn high and low were for peeing, not shredding! My paws were much too big for my body and caused me no end of grief, but other than that, my days were filled with wonder and awe.

It was my Dad who came up with the name Harry. My full name is Harry Cleveland Brown Howard, which has a nice ring to it if you happen to be as obsessed with American football as he is. Actually, we did hear of another Human recently who named his Golden

Wesley Welker, after the New England Patriots' wide receiver, so I guess there are other football nuts around. Funny, with a football team as a namesake, you'd think I'd show some interest in the game, but I never really  have—other than sniffing the ball occasionally to keep my Dad happy.

I think it's essential that you start off with an informed idea of the journey you are about to embark on—on the right paw, so to speak. So I need to set the record straight by assuring you there is nothing feigned, invented or imagined in any of the stories I am about to tell. They are all true, based on actual events. I know this better than anyone, because I was there as the central player in my own life and a participant and/or observer in the lives of everyone around me. What follows is an oath attesting to this:

I, Harry Cleveland Brown Howard, being of sound mind and body, do solemnly swear that the stories I am about to tell are the truth, the whole truth and nothing but the truth, so help me Dawg. Signed and sealed this 22nd day of December, 2001, at Ho Chi Minh City, Vietnam.

_____   _____
Harry Cleveland Brown Howard   *Brie Howard (witness)*

Done! Now I can begin in earnest!

* * *

I've been on the go since 1995, when I first landed in Hong Kong on the cusp of Typhoon Faye, which came in directly after us from Taipei. It was early July, the beginning of typhoon season, and from the moment the plane started falling out of the sky, and I mean plummeting straight down at an indescribable rate, I knew I was in for some big challenges. Thankfully, I've discovered a number of ways to make my moves easier, but trust me, life as an expat, canine or otherwise, is not for the faint of heart.

I think the most important lesson any of us can learn is to adopt a laid-back, go-with-the- flow approach to our new situation as soon as we hit the ground. Fortunately, it's second nature to Goldens, so we're luckier than most, including the snooty little Poodle we met in Hanoi, who spent every waking moment yapping at the beautiful ladies in their conical hats working in the rice fields, oblivious to the fact that the fruit of their labor was putting food into her ridiculously small stomach.

"When in Rome, do as the Romans do," meaning "eat every single thing the locals do, plus anything else you come across," is something we learned from our Humans, who tell everyone they swear by it, then turn around and gag at delicacies like boiled pig's tongue, squid's teeth, white ants' eggs, deep-fried grasshoppers and black chicken feet, in the next breath. Go figure. And speaking of chicken feet, I should mention the live catch we have scurrying through our house 24/7, namely geckos. Brie's favorite pastime in Vietnam is scouring the upper reaches of the walls for these cagey little creatures, then waiting for the precise moment to leap up and snag her catch.

Distractions are a Dawgsend at the best of times but a lifesaver when you're fresh off the plane, full of nostalgic thoughts of home and all the friends you've left behind, like Griffey, my very best canine friend; Sara, my Human sister; Crunch, my Mom's zany brother, and Big Joe, my Dad's Dad and the closest Human friend I've ever had. The sooner you can start looking for these the better, as far as I'm concerned, and it doesn't matter what they are as long as they take

your mind off things and keep you from sliding into a funk known as culture shock.

The problem is you're so jet-lagged at this point you can barely remember your own name, much less think about venturing into foreign territory in search of some exotic fish sauce to roll in. Not to worry. There'll be plenty of time for creativity once you get your feet on the ground—way better to stick to old standbys at first, things you're comfortable with, like paper shredding, for example, which has gotten me through almost all my initial slumps. Not only does it provide a diversion, it's enormously appreciated by the movers, who need all the help they can get once they start unpacking your boxes.

I mean, think about it. The past few days have been your worst nightmare ever: first, huddled in the farthest reaches of your kennel in Deep Dark Cargo of a 747 for hours, certain you wouldn't live to see the dawn; now, sprawled out on the floor of a strange, empty house, feeling more depressed than you've ever felt in your life. Anxious to put the whole ordeal behind you, you settle in for a nice long nap, only to be jolted out of a favorite dream by the deafening sound of the plane's engines still reverberating in your ears. Ever so slowly, you ease yourself into real time and take a quick reading on your surroundings. To your great relief, you discover you are no longer on the plane. You're back on terra firma, exactly where you were before the roar of the engines shattered your dream. Stretching out your legs as far as you possibly can, you yawn, let out a grateful sigh and attempt to drift off again.

Moments later, you're catapulted out of a Stage 1 of your snooze cycle by a tremendous brouhaha coming from outside: loud grating noises, wheels spinning, gears grinding, gravel spewing, something hissing and popping, an annoying series of beeps like the garbage truck in your old neighborhood used to make, alien tongues wagging and shouting and, finally, the hollow clank of your outside gate slamming shut. Somehow, you manage to drag yourself up off the floor and move in the general direction of the ruckus. When you reach the front porch, you see your Humans standing with glazed grins on their faces, waiting for something to happen at the rear of an enormous truck that's taken over your entire driveway and the new flower bed your Mom's been going on about since you arrived.

Wait a minute—it's the exact same truck you last saw pulling out of your driveway in Canada with all your stuff in it, and to your utter amazement, it's now sitting in your new one on the other side of the pond. And that's not all! The driver has just flung open the back door and the air is instantly filled with every scent you've ever known. You immediately abandon all self-control, fly down the steps as fast as you can and start racing around the garden in what can best be described as a loosey-goosey figure-eight formation, barking friendship and eternal gratitude to the movers. There's not a single doubt in your mind: before the sun goes down, your tennis balls, road-rageous raccoon, blankets, towels, kong, pig's ears, snack packs, sofa and Science Diet—all the things that make your life totally worth living—will be out of the cartons and at your disposal.

Boxes are already cascading out the back of the van one after another at a stupendous rate and making their way inside. The unpacking is about to begin, and you are squirming, twitching, wiggling and wagging with unspeakable excitement beside one carton whose contents you've already detected—your blankets, your plaid sleeping pad and what's left of your pillow after your last chew-a-thon. You'd know their smell anywhere.

It's nothing short of a miracle. You've barely moved a muscle in the past twenty-four hours and this Golden opportunity has landed on your doorstep, just like it always does, right down to the expression on the movers' faces when they see you getting primed for your paperwork. It's not a long-term project by any stretch of the imagination, but that's not important. All that matters is it will keep you busy enough to get through your first phase of culture shock.

And after the movers, who are no longer mere movers but your New Very Best Friends,[1] are done, you'll be completely occupied spending quality time with your Mom and Dad, who are going to be much needier than usual, owing to the combined stress and exhaustion of the move, which has finally caught up with them.

You can actually kill two birds with one stone at this point by running around your new house at optimum speed to get rid of your pent-up energy and barking and wagging your tail simultaneously to show your Humans how happy you are to simply *be* with them. But—a word of warning on this: You have to know when to stop! You'll sense a quiet sadness sweeping over the room, and the second you feel it, take half a beat to catch your breath, walk calmly over to the sofa and plunk yourself down at your Mom and Dad's feet. With your head resting between them, look mournfully into their eyes, sending a telepathic message to let them know you're there for them and you completely understand what they're going through, because this is no picnic for you either.

---

1 Because a huge part of Harry's life are his old friends, both Humans and canine, and the countless new ones he meets along the way, from this point on, he will describe them as his N(new)Fs, NVB(very best)Fs, NVBC(canine)Fs, and VBFs.

Odds are you'll end up sticking pretty close to home until they get through their first round of culture shock and become a little less frazzled, though they're going to be that way until they get some basic survival skills under their belts—like communicating, for starters. Not a problem. You can generally find enough diversions in your garden to keep you busy until they get back on their feet again. Brie and I spent our early days in Ho Chi Minh City digging trenches in the garden, which turned into an ongoing project, exceeding our expectations by a long shot. Deflowering hibiscus bushes was something else we took to right away, though it's an on-again, off-again sort of thing. A lot of distractions tend to be that way, so it's pretty much a lifetime mission to always be on the lookout for new ones.

When your Mom, who's your number one running partner, is feeling a little better and has some of the local language under her belt, which will consist mostly of hand gestures and three or four monosyllabic words strung together in short, choppy phrases spoken in a shrill, bordering on hysterical, tone (e.g., "*How* I go? *When* taxi come? *No, same same!* I tell you ten time... *same same different*"), she'll be ready to get rid of a little pent-up energy herself and at long last, you'll venture outside your gate for the very first time. Your biggest disappointment will be that you're going to be kept on a fairly tight rein until you can convince her that you're able to "handle your new situation," so lunging at the *bánh mi* lady's baguettes and diving for rice and noodles are simply not on at this stage. It will take all the restraint you can muster to hold back, but speaking with the voice of experience, the more control you can exercise during this trial period, the sooner your day of freedom will come.

Something I forgot to mention earlier about distractions is that some of the old ones you put aside when something better came along have this way of resurfacing unexpectedly, forcing you to drop what you're doing and deal with them on the spot, no matter what. It's hard to fathom because there can be a time lag of up to a week, and you can be perfectly happy doing whatever you're doing without the slightest intention of moving on to something else, when BOINK! This signal suddenly goes off in your brain and you find yourself flying to the opposite end of the garden in search of a mango pit you abandoned last Tuesday when you heard the refrigerator door open.

Of all the lessons I've learned, I have to say the most difficult has been not to expect the same things to happen in the new places that happened in the old. It just doesn't work that way, and I'm pretty sure it's the same for our Humans, so it's very important to remember. The last thing you want to do is spend your entire life waiting for something that isn't going to happen. I mean, just think what a terribly sad and disappointed little puppy you'd be.

Take snow, one of the most magical things in my life so far. Now, I have heard my Humans say "nothing is impossible," which leads me to believe we *could* wake up to a blanket of snow in Ho Chi Minh City one day, especially with the wonky weather all over the place, but deep down I don't think it's going to happen. Whenever my Mom senses I'm feeling depressed about something, she runs her fingers through the fur on the back of my neck, then scratches behind my ears and says in her most soothing voice, "Harry, it's just not meant to be." And because I trust her with my life, I take her word for it; in fact, I've already decided it's actually a Dawgsend it doesn't snow in Ho Chi Minh City.

To get my "drift," take thirty seconds right now and imagine yourself smack in the middle of thousands of motorbikes flying through enormously busy intersections, carrying five or six Humans on the back, dawgs, pigs, gas tanks, refrigerators, ginormous sheets of glass, flats of eggs stacked higher than Brie can jump—you name it, and that's just for starters. In between come the swarms of bicycles and pushcarts, with their bamboo baskets chockablock with squawking chickens, ducks and roosters; giant sacks of rice; and more baguettes than you've ever seen in your life. Not to mention the rickety China-blue pickups loaded to the gills with crates of rotting onions and whatever else they have beneath their flapping canvases; cyclos (pedicabs) pedaled by weary old men who have traveled more miles than they care to count; broken-down carts dragged by young, lean, bare-chested boys soaked in sweat; a never-ending stream of yellow Vina taxis, swerving

here, there and every-
where; and to top it off, a
few disgruntled chickens
looking for a free range
far from the madding
crowd.

So…there you are,
in the heart of Chaos
Central, with the whole
incredible scene pictured clearly in your mind. Now, watch closely
while every one of those motorbikes, bicycles, pushcarts, trucks, taxis,
cyclos plus their occupants, the rogue chickens and a group of startled
Japanese tourists attempting to cross the street in the midst of the madness, fly into the traffic circle all at once—drifting, gliding, skidding
and sliding uncontrollably across the slick, icy pavement, Humans
and animals alike gazing in wide-eyed astonishment at the huge white
flakes falling from the sky! *Ôi trời ơi* is all I can say, translated "Oh
my Gawd" in Vietnamese.

As my Mom says, "Harry, it's just not meant to be."

And if you've felt the joy of autumn as you bounded carefree through
brilliant orange and yellow leaves on a clear, sunlit afternoon in mid-
October, you'll have to tuck those memories away too, because that's
all they'll ever be. I have to say, swallowing these disappointments is a
lot easier said than done, and even though you know what your Mom
says is true, hope springs eternal. Who knows? Maybe, just maybe,
one day the other Harry will swoop down with the entire Hogwarts'
Quidditch team and bring Ho Chi Minh City's first snowfall with him!

Thankfully, Brie and I have discovered a way to make these longings
more bearable. All it takes is a reminder to keep our memories tucked
away in a special spot inside so that we can pull them out whenever we
need to and use them in our dreams. A few quick *zzzzzzzzs* and in no
time flat we're charging along our favorite running trails in Vancouver
or chilling out on our back lawn with our Mom after a mega run.
Sometimes, when we're lying in that canine state of utter bliss, making

quirky little sounds of contentment, we hear our Mom and Dad's voices from afar.

"Don't you wonder what they're dreaming about?" they ask, and we think to ourselves, "If only they knew," because at that moment, we're a million miles away, bounding across snow-covered fields with pure white crystals lacing our tails and dotting our freezing-cold noses, a clean, icy spray spewing out behind us. And when we reach the other side, we disappear completely into a magical forest of evergreens, where shadows dance on snowy boughs and sunrays filter through twisted branches, casting light on crusty tracks where squirrels and raccoons have gone before us.

Now, there's a flip side to this as well, because there will always be some memories that come back to haunt you as nightmares, like my run-in with a Rottweiler in Chiangmai, which I'll get to later.

Something I haven't mentioned is that no two moves from country to country are ever the same, and every place you go is going to have its own set of challenges. It will get easier over time, but there will

always be things that unravel you. It's unavoidable when you've been dropped into terra incognita. Your Humans will be very quick to tell you, in a light-hearted manner, that "it's all part of this wonderful adventure of ours," even when it's something totally beyond anything you've ever experienced. Easy for them to say, but then again, they're not the ones who have to pull themselves out of the silt of the Sông Sài Gòn or switch from Thai to Vietnamese in the space of three days if there's any hope of getting milk bones. *You* are!

Expect the unexpected is all I'm saying, and it's going to include some unbelievably off-the-wall behavior from your Mom and Dad, because of their own feelings of isolation and alienation. Trust me. You'll be amazed. The smallest, most insignificant incident can send them right off the rails; in fact, I think I'd better run through the different stages of culture shock so you won't be caught off guard. The timing and symptoms are generally the same for all new arrivals no matter where they come from.

Stage One, commonly referred to as the Honeymoon Stage:

As soon as they hit the ground, your Mom and Dad are going to be totally gobsmacked. There will be NOTHING they don't love: the sights, the sounds, the smells, the people, the shops, the service, the taxis, the weather, the supermarkets for aliens—Whoops! I mean foreigners—and the food at restaurants; as long as they're listed in this little book they won't leave home without—something like *Early Warnings of Culture Shock: A Handy Guide for Expats*.

Everything's basically perfect; it's all falling into place. My Mom's NVBF is the real estate lady, who finds us our house and gives her a signed copy of *Early Warnings*, and another extremely close acquaintance is her contact at the shipping company, who she phones five or six times a day, even though my Dad keeps telling her there's no point. "He'll be in touch when everything's cleared," he says for the umpteenth time, but she doesn't hear him. When he finally does call to let them know the truck will be arriving the next morning, they're completely over the moon, and when it actually pulls up in front of the house and the boxes start coming inside, it's all they can do to contain themselves. My Dad hooks up the stereo as soon as it comes out of the crate, and within minutes, the two of them are flying around like whirling dervishes with their favorite tunes blaring in the background. You have to see it to believe it!

My day is spent going through the huge volume of paperwork that has to be attended to (i.e., shredded) and racing from room to room to see what's coming out of the cartons and make sure nothing's been left inside. So by late afternoon, when the movers have left and the sun is pink and sinking lower in the sky, I couldn't do one more thing if my life depended on it, though it's a different kind of exhaustion than my usual drop-dead tiredness after a busy day—more of a dozy detachment.

Anyway, time to mosey back into the living room, drape myself over my favorite sofa and run through the highlights of the day to keep from falling asleep before dinner. It never ceases to amaze me. Our old house has literally dropped into our new one, and everything's exactly like it was.

Stage Two, also known as the Anger/Hostility Stage:
This stage of culture shock is by far the longest and most difficult

for our Humans. Luckily, this doesn't ring true for dawgs, though we feel deeply for our Mom and Dad and try to help them as much as we can. Like Stage One, the timing and symptoms are pretty much the same for most expats.

The honeymoon doesn't last. It can't. It would be far too much to expect having just landed on another planet. Up to this point, my Mom especially has been cruising along on this sort of dreamy, unnatural high—phoning her NVBFs a million times a day, sauntering around our new flat trying this here and that there, taking me out to acclimatize and poking around the neighborhood. But there's something I've noticed that's very unlike her. She hasn't gone out once to do things she "has to do," like she's done almost every single day since I was a puppy.

"Harry," she'd say when we were in Canada, "I'll be back in a while. I absolutely have to do blah, blah and blah (?!!?) before your Dad gets home," as if all hell would break loose if she didn't. Sometimes, she'd have this crumply piece of paper with writing scrawled all over it so that she wouldn't forget anything. But every time we land in a new country, she's stopped dead in her tracks. She'll head out to do whatever she intends to and reappear a few minutes later, looking completely and utterly defeated. It's hit her! She doesn't have a clue how to do it or even where to go to get it done. And it's not just one thing—it's a whole bunch of things she used to do be able to do in her sleep. This sudden realization sends her reeling into Stage Two.

She tries to put on her bravest face for as long as she can, pretending everything's fine, telling people how much fun she's having crossing the street with all the motorbikes trying to kill her; attempting to figure out when the lady at the market or the people cooking at restaurants are using these things with long leg bones that *look* like chickens but aren't (i.e., lizards, toads, rats and frogs); and getting lost and trying to make herself understood in a language that bears no resemblance to anything she's ever heard.

My Dad slips into his office routine fairly quickly, so Stage Two of culture shock doesn't hit him quite as hard, but don't get me wrong, he takes a few steep plunges too. I think it's because in their old life all they had to do was go with Step 1, Step 2 and Step 3. Done! *Finito!* Bada bing, bada boom! Zee-ro thought required! They try using the same technique they always have with a very simple task, but it doesn't work. It's not *same same,* and confusion, anxiety and frustration wash over them.

The only thing Brie and I can do is stay close. Sometimes, we just chill out for the afternoon by curling up on the bed and watching a DVD, except before long we're all zzzzzzzzing. Trust me—there's no way any of this is easy on the nerves, with things coming at you all at once and your senses being assaulted from every direction. Some days we're so exhausted, we can barely drag ourselves up the stairs.

After one of our Stage Two down times, our Dad tries to cheer us up with a few words of encouragement so that we won't keep spiraling down until we reach rock bottom. "Don't you worry now," he says in this slow, pandering, honey-tongued voice I've never heard before, "We're going to be *just* fine. One day at a time. We don't have to rush it. We knew what we were in for when we came, didn't we?" (We did? Whoops! Must have missed that one). He also has these rules for "Making it in Asia" that he loves to rattle off at will. My favorite is: "Have a sense of your own well-being," which I interpret as: Make sure you get your a.m. and p.m. snoozes in, especially when you're feeling totally disconnected.

Brie and I are lucky because we don't have to learn to do things differently like our Mom and Dad, for the simple reason that they do everything for us. But they don't have anyone to help them—they have to do it all themselves, and it completely overwhelms them. Every time they turn around there's another problem that wasn't a problem before we moved, because they knew what to do without even thinking about it and now they don't. Not only are they unsure of themselves and how to cope with day-to-day dilemmas (e.g., whether to smile or shake a paw when they meet someone, how to buy things at the market or how to ask for help when they need it), they're confused by their new Humans. People say yes when they mean no, smile when they're sad and make promises they don't keep. Just making a phone call or going to pick something up at a shop house[2] on our street can turn into a mega crisis. It's unbelievable and it's never-ending.

There's the dong (Vietnamese currency) that they can't figure out for the life of them, the man at the post office who says there's too much writing on their postcards and won't let them buy stamps and the lady at the bank who tells them "Passport no good ID," then goes berserk and starts yelling at the top of her lungs. The first time my Mom went to get her hair groomed in Hanoi, the lady did one side and went for lunch. She couldn't stop crying when she came home and I know it was because it was just all too much. Brie and I sat with her on the front porch right through our naptime, and later that day, she went back and had the other side cut.

Every day it's shopping troubles, phone troubles, house troubles, taxi troubles, worries about food, water, toilets, red bumps on their skin, cockroaches in the kitchen, snakes in the garden, bats, rats, paying too much or too little, being robbed or cheated—it doesn't stop. They may even be struck with the horrifying thought that the whole move was a terrible mistake and they can't believe they left Canada, "where everything really was perfect!"

Another thing I've noticed is that they've become far less trusting than they used to be, claiming that the new Humans are trying to "take advantage of them (?!!?) because they're *người nước ngoài,*"—translation, "Humans living outside their country"—or that the water and food are dirty when they're not. Anyway, you absolutely cannot forget that it's your job to *be there* for them, and it's not easy because you're going to see some of the weirdest behavior you've ever seen from your Mom and Dad, who you always thought were pretty normal as far as Humans go. There are these little mood swings called "outbursts" that are so unlike them, and the most amazing thing is that they can happen anywhere,

---

2 A two- or three-story building with a shop on the ground floor and living space behind and on the upper floors.

anytime—during your morning run, in the middle of your a.m. or p.m. nap, at breakfast or dinner, on the street, in a shop, at the bank and lots of times with people who come to fix things at your house, like the telephone man who can't get the phone to work "without the PO-LEECE radios cutting in" or the gas men who follow each other all over the place like little rabbits—twitching their noses and sniffing everywhere but still can't smell the gas that my Dad says "has to be coming from somewhere, but then again, they smell it all day long, so it's perfectly normal for them!"

One of the worst danger zones is in the back of taxis when they're trying to explain where they want to go. They're all right when they first get in, giving the driver instructions in a reasonably calm voice, pronouncing the place they want to go how they *think* it should be pronounced (i.e., WRONG) and waiting patiently for him to pull out and head in the right direction. But he doesn't. He just sits there. They try again, cranking up the volume to a hysterical level, using the same pronunciation (i.e., WRONG AGAIN), and before long, they have a full-blown situation on their hands. (Generally speaking, their reactions are way out of proportion to the root cause.)

Taxi drivers trigger a lot of their mini meltdowns, with their refusals to take them somewhere because they "no have time" or "too big traffic," to which my Mom responds in her strident voice, "*You* taxi driver. *You* have many many time, and traffic *you* job!" before getting out and flagging down another. For some reason, her speech has deteriorated a lot over the years, which is quite worrisome seeing as she's an English teacher.

There have been a few major meltdowns that have required a massage immediately afterward and/or a promise of a weekend away in the very near future—one following an eight-hour stint at Hong Kong Immigration, where my Mom had to listen for her number to be called above the jabber of hundreds of Filipino *amahs*, and another after standing in a queue in the post office in Hanoi for an entire morning, waiting to pick up a parcel from Canada, only to discover it was open and empty. That one was a major disappointment for Brie and me, because it was some dawg biscuits a man named Jeff had sent to us. My Dad said he hoped the man in the green suit and hat with the red star on it ate them for lunch. Go figure!

The closest we've come to a full breakdown was when my Mom slipped on a cow's entrails at Dong Xuan Market in Hanoi and had to go to the hospital to get her foot bandaged. I thought we might be heading back to Canada after that one, but we're still here.

Some things are so confusing that you, your Humans and most of the other Human expats you come across, will never understand them. How do you deal with these? You don't! You put them right out of your mind and pretend they never happened. Take *su'a chua*. It means "yogurt" AND "bicycle repair shop" in Vietnamese, depending on how it's sung, and who ever heard of a singing language? You don't want to go there. Ignore.

Stage Three, the Acceptance Stage:

At long last and with great relief, Stage Three finally arrives. It can mean one of two things. Either you've been in Asia too long and are out of touch with reality, or you've crossed over and gone "bamboo," which is Human mumbo jumbo for "going native." For your Humans, who have been struggling with severe mood disorders for some time, this stage is like a breath of fresh air, because a lot of the things that have been overwhelming for them become *almost* normal.

A sure sign that I've crossed over is that the curious, often "beyond belief," things I've been seeing since we arrived don't seem so strange anymore; in fact, I hardly even notice them. Example: When we first arrived in Vietnam, I went completely berserk every time I saw these enormous Brahma bulls wandering down our street all by themselves, but after a while I got used to it. They seem to come with the territory, and the truth of the matter is that they fend quite well on their own. There's one that comes by our house every afternoon after our nap, stops in front of the shop house where a lot of Humans, including my Dad, play pool, nudges around a little and moseys on his way, and no one even bats and eye. There are some other strays we see on our way to the river that my Mom calls "no-mad cows." I think they're different from the mad cows that have caused problems someplace else.

There was this expat German Shepherd we knew in Hong Kong who gave up all his creature comforts and went bamboo just like that—strolled out the door one day and never came back. Now he roams the untamed hills of Hong Kong Island with a pack of wild dawgs just like him. We used to hear them howling at night, but we never saw them during the day, which was a huge relief for me and all the other expat canines in our neighborhood.

We don't have a car in Vietnam, and we don't go in one very often, unless we have to go to the vet or our Mom and Dad decide to take us for a spin in a Vina taxi. In Hanoi, the vet was at the university, and we had to go quite often, which wasn't a particularly good thing. His name was Dr. Die, a little depressing when you think about it, but he was very kind and worth a lot to us. They don't say "doctor" in Vietnamese like they did in Canada and Hong Kong; they say *"docteur."* My Mom says it's *"très* French," like *bonjour, madame* and *baguettes.*

My Mom goes almost everywhere on the back of a *xe ôm,* which is a motorcycle taxi, and every once in a while, she takes cyclos. There's nothing Brie and I would love more than to be zooming around Ho Chi Minh City with her, but there's no way it's going to happen—not with all the madness out there. Lots

of times she's too afraid to even cross the street, so she waits for a Vietnamese Human to come and take her by the hand.

My Dad's always talking about "Zenning it." "Just ease your way out into the chaos," he tells her, "and let the insanity flow around you." But I can see she's clearly not ready for it. She says it's like the Wild West, except she calls it "the Far East." There are quite a

31

few things our Humans go on about that we really don't understand, which is probably what most Dawgs say about their Humans.

But one thing we do understand is that these moves aren't nearly as easy for them as they are for us and we have to make absolutely sure we're there for them when the reality check hits them full force, bringing with it countless problems they have no idea how to deal with. I actually think Stage Two is like a make-it-or-break-it crisis stage, because my Mom and Dad knew this lady who wouldn't go outside her house after the honeymoon was over—just stayed inside crying all the time and eventually had to go back to Canada for good. Thankfully for our Humans *and* for us, their mini outbursts and melt-downs usually let up when they get more used to the language (if that's what you want to call it), the Humans and the customs of our new country. One of the first signs that they're getting better is that they start to smile and laugh again, and I mean totally crack up, at things that drove them crazy in the beginning. Go figure.

Anyway, if I hadn't seen and experienced all that I have firsthand, I probably wouldn't believe a lot of it myself, but I've sworn under oath that all my stories are true, and I'll stick to that until the day I die. And if I'm going to give you the best account possible, which is what I've set out to do, I'll have to go back to the very beginning so you'll understand how it all came to be.

CHAPTER 2
From Puppyhood to the Outer Limits

My earliest memories are of my Humans, my new home and the Dawg Park, where I could go with my Mom and Dad to meet other puppies and stay off lead for hours and hours. The ocean was at my feet and the mountains at my back, with millions of fluffy green Dunlops in between, which is how I imagine Dawg heaven!

I loved my Humans as soon as I met them, and I knew they loved me, because they smothered me with hugs and kisses 24/7—and they weren't the only ones! I guess it's the soft, cuddly nature of puppies that makes everyone want to pick them up and hold them against their chests. I'd lick their faces, nip at their ears and chew on their collars, which always made them deliriously happy.

I also loved lying quietly on my Mom and Dad's laps, feeling their warmth and taking in their scent while they scratched behind my ears. My Mom's was soap and shampoo, mingled with delicious aromas that floated out of our kitchen and a wide range of easily detectable household odors, like sofas and chairs, the vacuum and clean laundry. My Dad's was altogether different but the same as most Human Dads I've encountered—a blend of wet towels, sweat, aftershave, leather, newspapers, the garage and the inside of our car.

Instead of reading the newspaper every morning like my Humans did, I'd sniff everything I came across, and then commit the scents to memory. Most were distinct enough for me to pick up easily the next time; others were more complex and took longer to figure out. Of course, a steady stream of brand-new, unfamiliar smells jumped out at me every day, and although some went directly into my database, others would drift off and go undetected forever. For me, the strangest were the intangibles—things like fear and danger that you never dreamed you could smell, yet you knew them instinctively. Rather than skip by lightly on a gentle breeze, they lingered and hung heavily in the air.

I came to know my Humans better with each passing day and watched their odd routines with curiosity and fascination. In the mornings, my Dad would put white soapsuds all over his face, then scrape them off with a silver knife, while my Mom stood next to him holding a wind machine that made her hair blow.

If we went to a busy shopping area, they'd usually carry me, but I'd wear my leash so that they could put me down to widdle or accommodate the countless Humans who wanted to pat me. Sometimes, I'd look up to see an enormous giant towering over me with rough hands that magically transformed the moment they reached down and ruffled my fur. Other times, I'd hear a child calling out, "Mommy, puppy, puppy!" and feel the delicate touch of tiny fingers moving tentatively along my back. No matter who it was, their attention elicited a response I had no control over. I'd feel a burst of joy and my tail would start wagging furiously, all by itself.

When I first started exploring the garden, I'd run around the perimeter, sniffing and peeing all over the place to mark my territory. For some reason, it made me feel more comfortable about where I was. I still do it every time we move, but once I've acclimatized, I don't do it nearly as much. I protect my inside space by scratching and pawing neurotically on a special spot on my sofa or the floor before I settle in for a nap. Whenever I do it, my Mom and Dad look at me strangely, but it doesn't bother me because I totally trust my instincts.

I could feel myself growing by leaps and bounds, which made climbing stairs and scrambling up onto beds much easier. I got to know most of the dawgs I played with at the Dawg Park and would greet them like best friends, though I wasn't exactly sure what best friends were. We'd run and wrestle and jump in and out of the water, barking at the sky and the gulls until it was time to go our separate ways. The next time I went back, I'd be on the lookout for friends I'd played with the last time but it was hit and miss, and sometimes we never saw each other again.

From the very first day my Humans brought me home, they knew I absolutely lived for car rides. So if we were going somewhere, my Dad would let me scramble into the back seat and wait until they were ready, which always took longer than I expected. One day, they said we were going "to meet a new friend named Griffey," who lived on the other side of the big bridge. After we'd gone through the park and busy streets, over a smaller bridge, past a beach and up a long, steep hill, we pulled into a long driveway with a huge expanse of tall, green, feathery trees and beautiful blue and purple flowering bushes everywhere. The front door was open and as soon as we were out of the car, a dawg about my size came bounding toward us with his Humans in tow. They greeted my Mom and Dad with smiles, hugs and the usual guffaws Humans insist on every time they see each other. Finally, there was a short pause to catch their breath and give Griffey's Dad a chance to say something. "Time to introduce the dawgs," he announced with a huge grin on his face. "Griff, Harry. Harry, Griffey." Nicely low key compared to my Mom's gushes to total strangers that they "simply have to meet" her "beauty boy," but she can't help herself!

Griffey was a black-and-white Border Collie, whose obsession with squirrels was almost as bad as mine was with tennis balls. And like me, he owed his name to his Dad's sports addiction, except it wasn't football; it was baseball. His all-time favorite players' names were Griffey and Griffey (?!!?). Anyway, the fact that our Dads were crazy enough about sports to choose our names from their favorite teams and players was probably what created the friendship between us. Griffey didn't seem to have much interest in his Dad's game either, but at least he could get his teeth into the ball.

The rest is history. It was instant camaraderie between Griffey and me. We indulged in a few token sniffs front and rear before we planted our paws and arched our backs—priming ourselves for takeoff. In the next breath, we were running around the garden in wide, sweeping circles, chasing each other through the trees and jumping over the flower beds, coming to a screeching halt every few rounds just long enough to change directions.

When we couldn't go one more lap if our lives depended on it, we flopped down on our backs, panting and rolling in the grass in pure ecstasy. Later, we went for a long walk with our Humans through Griffey's neighborhood. The air was cooling off and smelled of dry leaves on the ground and smoke billowing from people's houses. When we left, the hazy sunlight was fading into twilight, and by the time we got home, it was almost dark. Two profound thoughts went through my brain as I lay on the back seat of the car mulling over my day. Griffey was the most awesome dawg I'd ever met. He was also my first ever VBCF!

Max and Riley were my other VBCFs, and Griffey's, too. They were incredibly strong Labrador Retrievers, and we'd all run together in Pacific Spirit Park, with its towering trees rising up from the forest floor, their canopy providing shade and creating a mist that cooled my muzzle. On clear days, the sun would filter through and play with the shadows, and when it got colder, the air was so clean it made my eyes water.

I'll never forget the day we drove to the mountains and I saw snow for the very first time. I'd never seen anything so strange and fresh and beautiful. It was cold and crisp and crunchy underfoot and made my paws feel all pink and tingly. When I rubbed my nose in it, I could taste it, and it was unlike anything I'd ever tasted before. Pure white snow that fell from the sky and melted on your tongue. Imagine! Some things are simply too amazing to comprehend!

It was early in my life and purely by accident when I discovered the generous nature of not only my own Humans but Humans in general. I was sitting in the kitchen one afternoon, watching my Mom while she was making dinner. Every so often, she'd glance down and see me staring up at her. This went on for some time, and finally she laughed and handed me a piece of chicken from the pot. We went through the same thing repeatedly—gaze for gaze—and miraculously, a little morsel appeared at regular intervals. BOINK! A light suddenly went on, and I was as certain of my chance discovery as I was of the sun coming up in the morning. If I sat there staring at her in awe like I'd been doing for Dawg knows how long, I could get *almost* anything I wanted! When my Dad came home that night, I tried it with him, and again the next day with Louisa at my pet store. The results were exactly the same. To my astonishment, I discovered it also worked with perfect strangers. It's been a revelation to me ever since.

My Human sister, Sara, says our Mom and Dad are "obsessed" with Brie and me and rolls her eyes every time she has to listen to them going on ad nauseam about something they've read on a Golden calendar or retelling yet another "Day in the Life of Harry and Brie." One of our Mom's favorite quotes, which she used to reel off to everyone she met when I was a puppy, prefacing it with "It's so Harry," is still in bold letters on our refrigerator with a picture of me underneath: "He seemed neither old nor young. His strength lay in his eyes. They looked as old as the hills, and as young and as wild. I never grew tired looking into them."—John Muir.

Ho hum…you now know my Mom!

I cohabited with a cat named Chibi, who was an expat when my Mom and Dad lived in Japan. "Chibi" actually means "little" in Japanese, but he was one humungous cat, although it didn't seem to bother him that his name didn't suit him anymore. He was a pretty awesome cat, with a casual, kind of bohemian, way about him. He could have come by it honestly, but I think he picked up a lot of it in Tokyo, because he lived near this funky area called Harajuku. My Humans describe it as "a strange mixture of punk rock, Hello

Kitty, and anime" (?!!?).The only word I recognize in that entire spiel is "kitty," which is what they called Chibi in very high-pitched voices when they wanted him to come inside. I guess it was his middle name, as in Chibi Kitty Howard, not unlike Harry Cleveland Brown Howard, except I've never heard them singing, "Here, Cleveland Brown. Come on, Cleveland Brown," not once, even though they tell everyone it's my real name.

Anyway, old Chibi sure loved fish. My Mom and Dad were always telling people his taste became "more refined from living in Japan," which was why he turned up his nose at his Whiskas canned food. It could sit around in his dish from morning till night without him so much as walking past it. If nothing better came along, he eventually ate it, but by the time he did, the color and texture were beyond description. But trust me, this was definitely not the case with Japanese takeout. Chibi got all the leftovers, and I swear they were gone before he drew his next breath! I have to admit I was bothered by my Mom and Dad's assumption that Chibi, being a cat, was synonymous with fish and Harry, being a dawg, with meat, kibble and garbage. Their conclusion: I wouldn't like sushi. Hullo! Where exactly did that come from? I mean, it wasn't like I'd changed. I've always eaten anything.

Chibi's other passion was birds. He'd bring them inside and deposit them at the foot of Sara's bed at least once a week. If we had guests, he'd leave his trophy *on* the bed as opposed to *beside* it, as a gesture of true hospitality. When I first went out for walks on my leash, Chibi would trot along behind us, more like a dawg than a cat, but when my Mom started taking me for runs, he stayed home and just came for our after-dinner strolls.

As a puppy, I was a ball of energy and loved doing pretty much anything as long as it kept me busy. Some of my early pastimes turned out to be pure puppy dawg antics that eventually fell by the wayside, even though I go back to them occasionally for the sheer love of being

a puppy all over again: chasing my tail until I got dizzy, hopping up the stairs then rolling down, and chewing or shredding whatever I could get my little piranha teeth into. Of course, if something smelled like my Humans, it got top priority no matter what it was. Whoops! That's not entirely true. Their "intimates" were definitely a notch above the rest.

Other activities stayed with me and bring me as much joy now as they did then—things I never grew tired of and do whenever the spirit moves me or the opportunity presents itself, like flying around in circles inside and out of the house for no other reason than feeling happy to be alive; digging holes in the backyard; collecting leaves in my fur; going to get the paper after a snowfall, though that one had to be put on the back burner because there's no snow in Ho Chi Minh City; rolling on the carpet or the grass; shredding my tennis balls; going for car rides; running and playing with Humans and other dawgs; having my ears scratched and my tummy rubbed; taking long walks and longer naps; watching TV, especially Discovery Channel and tennis; eating pretty much anything and everything; and last but not least, making NVBFs. I should emphasize that besides loving my Humans more than anything in the world, making NVBFs is the second most important thing in my life.

One of my biggest thrills of all was when I first started running with my Mom. The feeling was unlike anything I'd ever experienced: fresh air, freedom, love and joy all rolled into one. We'd set out early in the morning, when the air was crisp and sharp and the ground was damp with dew, running side by side, taking in everything around us: the sky, the earth, the grass; the smell of woodpiles and autumn, of spring or summer and breakfasts wafting out of our neighbors' kitchens.

The minute I saw her putting on her shoes, excitement would stand up inside me, then charge through my body like an electric current, and there was no way I could contain it. I'd be instantly transformed into this goofy flurry of fur, jumping and prancing in circles in front of the door, flinging my head from side to side, whipping my tail back and forth and nudging up against my Mom to get going. Once I got the hang of it, I'd take one end of my leash in my mouth, and she'd take the other. Then off we'd go, running in perfect harmony, a duo of happiness.

When I was about nine months old, I went to school with a few other dawgs, mostly puppies. I already knew how to heel, but I learned to sit, come and lie down *most* of the time. The teacher was a very big lady with an enormous shelf across her chest. My Dad thought "she was probably a sergeant in the British army before she started teaching obedience classes" (?!!?). Whatever her past life had been, she instilled the fear of Dawg in everyone, including my Mom and Dad, and my success came only as a result of the holy terror I felt every time her voice boomed out a command.

Around this same time, my Mom and Dad started talking in muffled voices about "Hong Kong" and after I heard the words the first time, they kept popping up in hushed conversation over dinner or whenever they were talking into the phone. Then, one morning while I was doing my rounds in the garden, sniffing the flowers, kicking dirt onto the grass and screaming across the lawn after Chibi, this monstrous van appeared out of nowhere and parked itself smack in the middle of our driveway. From the moment that truck arrived and the packers descended on us, chaos invaded every single room of our house and it wasn't until our whole life had been turned completely upside down; packed into hundreds of boxes; and pushed, shoved and crammed into the rear of the truck that a sense of calm returned. But even then, it wasn't a sense of calm as we'd known it. The only things left in the house were my kennel and a few suitcases, and I felt incredibly lonely lying beside them in the kitchen, listening to the hollow sound of footsteps on the bare floors and voices echoing throughout the house. The next thing I knew, my Dad was gone, too, and I had to sleep at Mac's house, who I'd only met once before, but it was okay with me, seeing as Mac was as crazy about tennis balls as I am.

I was still sleepy the morning Captain Crunch, my Mom's zany brother, came to pick us up to take us to the airport. He jumps at any chance he gets to go near planes, especially when it's with us and we're flying clear across the Pacific. He's into something called "airline memorabilia," which means he collects all the stuff from planes that he can get his hands on: airline safety cards, airsick bags, used cutlery, in-flight magazines—pretty much anything that has an airline logo on it, and the older the better. My Mom says he's "eccentric, and there's nothing wrong with that."

Anyway, after he's accumulated quite a lot, he goes to meetings to trade with other zany people who are interested in the same sort of junk. Whoops! Sorry, sorry, Crunch. I didn't mean junk; I meant "stuff." I guess it's like: "Tell you what, Harry. I'll give you one of my Cathay Pacific safety cards, plus two of my Ethiopian Air throw-up bags, if you give me one of your Dragonair in-flight magazines." Crunch is always happy about his big-time scores, especially his huge model planes that have "Lufthansa" or "Japan Airlines" written on the side. He keeps some in the trunk of his car, just in case movie companies want to use them on a set. When you go to his house, you can hardly move for the boxes. I mean, it's pretty weird when you think about it. My Mom just shrugs her shoulders and says, "Different strokes for different folks," and I think to myself, "WHOA! She's sure got that one right!"

One time we brought Crunch an airsick bag from Lao Air, something my Dad says you have to keep handy "if you're going to fly with those lunatics." He's not one to mince his words. When my Mom was on her way back to Hanoi from Laos once, it was so foggy inside the plane she could barely see her hand in front of her face. I don't think she's flown Lao Air since.

Anyway, on the way to the airport my Mom kept apologizing, like she does, telling me how sorry she was that I had to check in so early.

My Humans always talk to me like that, as though I'm one of them. I think they forget dawgs aren't people, but that's okay because sometimes we forget we're dawgs. When she's going upstairs to do something like take a shower, she'll say, "Stay here, Hars, I'll be down in a minute," as if I'd actually consider not following her and waiting in the bathroom until she's finished. It can be totally exhausting—up and down, up and down, umpteen times a day!

When we got to the airport, Captain Crunch pulled up in front of a huge building, where we waited until a man came and put my kennel onto a truck and drove it to an exceptionally wide road where there was an enormous plane and a lot more noise than I was accustomed to. I stayed there beside the plane for what felt like two hundred million hours.[3] Then I was on the truck again, heading Dawg knows where. When they lifted me off, I was rolled into a warm, cozy office where, to my surprise and relief, my Mom was waiting.

Whatever we were doing had been "dee-layed," so she stayed there, sitting on the floor beside me, patting me softly and repeating in her most soothing voice, "It's okay, Hars. It's okay," while I lay there, motionless with my head on her lap, gazing into her eyes for reassurance. After a while, she kissed me on my forehead and settled me back into my kennel, explaining it was time to go and she'd see me in Hong Kong.

I learned later that one of the men in the office told her I'd feel better if I had something with her scent with me. She disappeared for a few minutes and when she came back, she slipped something soft underneath my front paws. My Mom's bra traveled all the way to Hong Kong with me.

Right after she left, I was lifted onto the truck again and driven out to the plane, where I sat on the tarmac until it was time to be rolled up the ramp. When the door closed, I was plunged into total darkness. I listened. An eerie silence fell over everything like an icy calm,

---

3 Harry's understanding of time comes from his own inner clock, so any references he makes to time intervals as we know them are completely random. The same thing applies to his estimates of numbers of people and countable objects.

but the minute the power was switched on, the deafening sound of the engines took over the entire space around me.

The plane backed up, then began moving forward ever so slowly, and as soon as it did I slid into the deepest corner of my kennel, curled myself into a tight little ball and stayed there, afraid to move a single hair, my heart pounding and my head throbbing as the noise grew louder and louder. Suddenly, everything around me began rattling and shaking so violently I was certain the whole plane was about to break apart, and in the next breath, we were thundering down the runway at an indescribable rate, gathering speed and momentum—the roaring infinite, the vibrations charging through my body like a runaway freight train tearing down a track.

We must have reached top speed and the end of the runway at the same time, because there was a sudden *ga-lump* as the plane lifted off the ground and began its slow, labored climb, struggling against its own massive weight. The terrible shuddering continued, followed by an unexpected thud as something heavy came up underneath me. And all the time, I kept burrowing deeper and deeper into the folds of my blanket to try to block out the sound, but there was no way I could, because it was trapped right there with me in the underside of that 747 with no place else to go. I was certain my eardrums had shattered in two.

Now, I think I mentioned earlier that my Mom and Dad have a tendency to tell things differently than they actually are, which produces one of two results: events are either grossly underplayed or exaggerated beyond recognition. It's not that they deliberately set out to lie. They just elect to gloss over certain details to try to make things easier, or blow them out of all proportion to embellish their own stories later. In this case, it was the former—the old song and dance about having a "nice long sleep as soon as you get on the plane" and "being there for you when you get off." Trust me, neither of these is going to happen. First of all, in order to have that "nice long sleep," you have to get UP there. Second, "being there for you" would mean accompanying you on a Minivan Ride from Hell with a totally mad Chinese,

Thai or Vietnamese driver jabbering away on his cell phone with a two-way radio blaring in the background as he careens between ten hundred jumbos at whatever mega airport you happen to have landed at in an attempt to get you to Customs or your connecting flight in record-breaking time.

In all fairness, a viable excuse for not telling you everything is that they can't, for the simple reason that they haven't experienced it themselves. I know this for a fact, because when Brie and I were sitting in Bangkok on our way to Ho Chi Minh City, waiting to be rolled into Deep Dark Cargo, we saw our Mom getting off a bus and going up some stairs on the completely opposite side of the plane, which put her at least two floors above us, where she wouldn't have to contend with the earth-shattering noise and vibrations rumbling through her entire being. And that's only part of it! She was actually going up there to be with a whole cabin full of Humans who were already lying around in the lap of luxury under logoed blankets Captain Crunch would kill for, getting ready to eat fancy meals and watch movies on their own private TV screens. We're not even on the same plane here, if you get my drift. I've often wondered how well they'd cope being cooped up inside a kennel in Deep Dark Cargo, right next to the wheel bay where those enormous Bridgestones drop down and the engines and landing gear just happen to be!

The other reason they don't tell you the full story is that they want to reassure you as much as they can, and you can't fault them for this. They *are* genuinely worried about you. There's also a chance you can have that "nice long sleep" once you reach cruising altitude, as long as a little glitch called turbulence doesn't kick in. But odds are it will. Just when your nerves have begun to settle, the plane does this unexpected free fall right out of the blue, taking your brief moment of tranquility and the entire contents of your stomach down with it. Meanwhile, the rest of you is riveted to the floor, with the exception of every hair on your body, which is standing on end! At least the Humans upstairs get a warning when it's coming, though the captain, being Human himself, doesn't generally provide them with many details.

Back to that night when I was heading UP UP UP. I have to admit, something did happen when we got to a certain point. Maybe we'd reached the Outer Limits, because the plane wasn't climbing anymore and the noise became almost bearable. I even began to think that I might get that "nice long sleep" after all.

I drew in a deep breath and blew the air out as slowly as I possibly could, forcing all the tension down through my body and out the bottom of my paws, squeezed my shoulders blades together and took one more, letting it go with an enormous sigh. As soon as I closed my eyes, I felt a pleasant drowsiness coming over me, and it couldn't have been long before I drifted off into dreams of tennis balls and snow, towering trees and sunlight, and Griffey and my Mom and Dad.

CHAPTER 3
Hong Kong

When I floated off to that never-never land, a million miles away from where I'd ever been before, I didn't give a single thought to having to return to earth, until I was jolted back to reality by the sound of the engines speeding up and cutting back, the terrifying feeling of our sharp descent and the excruciating throbbing in my ears. A few deep breaths to try to stop the wild racing of my heart as the plane lowered and the power increased. The next thing I remember was a heavy clunk and a moment where it felt as though we were suspended in the air with some mysterious force holding us up from underneath, before the shuddering vibrations as we hit the runway hard. I slid sideways with the impact, feeling the same jarring shudders as the wheels bounced up and touched down again then rolled us forward, taking the full weight and momentum of that huge mass of metal screaming forward into the night.

When we hit the ground the second time, I was sure my life was about to come to a sudden and tragic end, but miracle of miracles, the awful squeal of the tires and the terrifying trembling and shaking gradually tapered off as the speed decreased and the plane began coasting smoothly down the runway. I felt my whole body begin to relax with the knowing feeling that we were back on terra firma and I was still in one piece. A brief pause and we were moving again, bouncing and lurching now and then with the brakes, then turning ever so slightly. Our pace had slowed to that of a tired old warrior returning home after a long, hard battle, which is exactly how it felt, because the whole ordeal was so horrific. Wheels rolling; the sound of the engines fading; the brakes again, pitching me forward; still moving. Then stop. I took a long breath in and let it go with a grateful sigh of relief.

My kennel rolled down the ramp into a wet, blustery night before being loaded onto a kind of pickup that sped across the wide road we'd come in on to the far end of a brightly lit building, the wind racing along with us, carrying sheets of water that lashed against the sides of the truck. When we came to a standstill, I was carried inside under cover and set down in what must have been an immense space with its loud, echoing sounds and unsettling noises: jangling voices nearby, different from my Mom and Dad's; loud clunks and thuds; the drone of machinery; engines starting and stopping; shrill, grating music coming from somewhere; a constant hum overhead; and the torrential rain pelting down relentlessly on the roof. A few Humans knelt beside me and pushed their fingers through the mesh of my kennel to touch my nose. I inched forward so that I could lick them, overjoyed by the warmth and comfort of Human contact.

They stayed there, crouching and smiling, until a minivan pulled up beside us, then helped the driver lift me up and strap me onto the seat. He immediately spun around, and we sped away from the glaring white of the airport into a maze of dark streets, illuminated every so often by streaks of green and yellow light bouncing off the shiny, wet pavement. When we stopped, I was loaded onto a cart, and rolled up a ramp through a darkened doorway into a building, then down a dimly lit hall into a room where my kennel was placed on the floor. The only thing I could see in front of me were the oddly angled legs of a rickety metal table, with piles of paper stacked loosely underneath. I detected a Human smell, but there were no voices, only the steady whirr of a ceiling fan overhead.

I'm not sure how long I lay there, wishing my Mom and Dad would walk through the door; I may have even drifted off. But suddenly, I heard footsteps and I knew immediately they were theirs. If ever there was a gift "scent" from heaven, it was my Mom and Dad's that night, and the sight and sound of them kneeling down to unlatch my kennel, rubbing my ears and speaking in soft, loving tones, telling me the worst was over.

Their strong protests that I had had a rabies shot just before we left were ignored as a lady in a dirty white coat walked briskly over to me, jabbed a needle into my backside, grabbed some papers and slid them across the table to a man slouched over a bowl, eating noodles. Without so much as a glance, he picked up a stamp, pounded it twice, tossed the papers onto the floor and went back to slurping. I don't know how many meals I'd missed, but I do remember feeling a pang in the pit of my stomach and having to resist the temptation to lunge clear

across the table. They could have been Shanghai noodles for all I know, like the ones Mr. Leung introduced me to a few weeks later. Mr. Leung looked after all the flats in our building, and after he'd finished his lunch every day, he'd give me his bowl to lick. He was my first VBF in Hong Kong. Oddly enough, when I was lying in the back seat of the car a few minutes later, with my head draped over my Mom's lap just the way I like it, those noodles were all but forgotten and my only thoughts were of home and feeling safe again.

The back door of the car was open and I could smell damp earth and hear my Mom's voice: "We're here, Hars." I must have fallen asleep. I could also hear dawgs, and I mean a lot of them, howling and wailing, even with the wind screaming and the rain pounding down harder than ever. Where were we and where was home? It couldn't be here. Not with all those woeful cries.

They took me inside, stopping briefly at a desk to talk to some Humans, and after a few minutes, we were led through a series of long, colorless hallways with stark rooms on either side. The doors were barred, but I could see dawgs inside:—more than I'd ever seen in my life, some pacing back and forth frenetically, others lying life-lessly on the floor, their heads pressed between their paws, their eyes dull and empty. Eventually, we stopped in front of a room with the door ajar. My kennel was carried in behind me and my Mom and Dad spread some towels and my blanket out beside my water bowl, then spoke to me quietly, massaging the creases of my neck and rubbing behind my ears.

"It's just for a little while, Hars, I promise," my Mom said. "Until our flat's ready. I'll be back as soon as I can tomorrow to take you for a nice long walk." Hugs from both of them, then they were gone, and I was left alone on the cold, hard floor. The howling never stopped, and all I could do was lie there, listening to the steady beat of the rain, trying as hard as I could to block out the painful cries, feeling my own heart racing and my nerves unraveling whenever there was an unexpected thunderclap or the rattle of a door that a desperate dog was jumping up against.

Time can play terrible tricks when you're in a strange place, alone and frightened out of your wits, with no idea why you've been left there or when your Humans will be back to take you home. As I lay there, listening to the frantic cries of those poor souls in captivity, longing for the sound of my Mom's footsteps and the reassurance of her voice, even the smallest sliver of time felt endless. But there was nothing I could do, except wait and give time however long it needed. True to her word, my Mom appeared the next afternoon, as soon as there was a break in the storm.

The day was still gloomy when we set out for our walk, with dark clouds moving quickly across the sky, but the thunder had stopped and the rain had turned to a light drizzle. We followed a soggy path up through the trees behind the kennels, and my spirits lifted as I bounced along beside her, taking in the moist air as deeply as I could and filling my lungs with the fresh smells of the earth after a rain. When we got back, she pleaded with a man to move me to a quieter spot, then settled me onto my blanket and sat with me for a while, rubbing my tummy. She looked sad when she left and said she couldn't believe "they allow birds in the Mandarin Oriental Hotel but won't take you, Har Bear," which is my all-time favorite nickname. Later that afternoon, the man came back and moved me around the corner, but it didn't make any difference. No matter how hard I tried, I couldn't block out the haunting sounds that echoed through Pok Fu Lam's dank halls.

The next morning my Mom came earlier and we walked for a long time, then sat outside at a bus stop before she reluctantly took me back. "I'm trying to figure this out, Har," she said with the same sadness in her voice. "And I will. I promise. Just give me a little more time."

On the third day, she was as bright and cheerful as I'd seen her since we'd arrived, and I was almost sure she'd come up with a plan. She brought a man in with her and asked him to bring my kennel with everything in it, then clipped on my leash, held my head in her hands, looking directly into my eyes, and whispered into my ear, "I couldn't stand it, Harry, not for one more second." I felt my whole body tingle with the indescribable feeling of knowing I was safe again and would be for a long time to come.

A big old taxi was waiting outside with the man who'd helped with my kennel, and he drove us to our new house on the south side of Hong Kong Island, except it wasn't called a house, it was called a flat, and it was what we'd been waiting for. It was in a low white building that faced directly out to the sea.

Everything we saw from our windows that day was the colors of the earth: a sea as blue as the sky and hills painted in a million shades of green, gold, brown and rust. And so for the next little while, my Mom and I camped out on the bare floor of our empty flat in Chung Hom Kok, sleeping side by side on a quilt looking out over the South China Sea, watching the sun go down and the silver twilight shimmer across the water, while my Dad stayed at the Mandarin Oriental Hotel—because he could! Some days, my Mom would go into town for dinner, and others, he would come to us. When a bed and futon were finally delivered, he came home for good.

Directly below us was a swimming pool strictly for Humans, and beyond it and to the east lay wilderness, most of it too thick to walk through. When we went out to acclimatize, which you have to do gradually so that you don't feel overwhelmed, we'd stick to the paths down to the beach or the road up to Chung Hom Kok hill. And every night at dusk, we'd walk to the bus stop and wait for bus number 6X to bring my Dad home from work.

Chibi didn't come with us; instead, he stayed with Sara. But after we'd been in Hong Kong for a while, he turned up with my Mom one day, completely out of the blue. He fell into his old routine right away, as if he'd been an expat living in Hong Kong all his life. Chibi was like that—he took everything in his stride. In the mornings, he'd go out to acclimatize, and after he got bored, he'd come back inside and badger me, then curl up on a floor cushion and stay there for the rest of the day, sleeping or just staring out the window at the South China Sea. Occasionally, he'd wander into the kitchen and jump up on top of the fridge or pad into the office so that he could lie on the computer. I think he was glad to be an expat cat again, but you were never really sure with Chibi. He wasn't one to bare his soul. Anyway, I was one happy camper to have him with us again, seeing as he was such a long-standing member of our family.

I don't know how many sleeps it was until the truck came with our things, but I do know we were the happiest family in Hong Kong the day it arrived, flying around our flat putting everything away until the last rays of sunlight had disappeared. When we'd gotten rid of the few remaining cartons, we sat down in the middle of the floor with a giant pizza that had come on the back of a motorbike. Everything was just as I remembered: my tennis balls, road-rageous raccoon, blankets, Chuckit, pull toys, pig's ears, snack packs, towels, sofa and enough Science Diet to open a Star Pets on Horizon Drive.

There are times in your life when it's almost impossible to express how happy you feel, because you simply can't imagine anyone feeling the way you do at that particular moment, which is how it was when "home" came to us in Hong Kong. If you'd been a fly on the wall later that night, you might have thought there was a tornado whirling through our flat, but on closer inspection, you would have discovered it was me, Harry Cleveland Brown Howard, newly arrived expat dawg, on my first overseas posting in Hong Kong.

* * *

The summer rains continued. Sometimes they'd fall as a misty drizzle or sudden showers from passing cloudbursts, but there were other times when everyone would rush home because a *taiphoon*[4] was "coming down." That's what they'd say—"It's coming down," as if it was this gigantic extraterrestrial body that was about to crash down on all of us from the Outer Limits, which wasn't very far from the truth when I thought about it.

Now, even though a lot of Human language is just plain old mumbo jumbo to us, and most of our understanding comes from Human body language and gestures, there are certain things besides our own names and the dawg commands we're "supposed" to learn that we pick up very easily. They come in different tones, and as soon as we hear them, we know exactly what they mean.

When you're a puppy, full of puppy dawg antics, or even a grown-up dawg who *should* know better, your Humans can sound a little stern, like when they tell you you're "a bad dawg" or "a real handful," but it doesn't happen very often. Mostly their tones are over the top with love and bursting with excitement and anticipation, but there are a few you hear once in a while that make your nerves jump and your heart skip a beat. "Typhoon" was like that. Whenever the word was spoken, you knew there was imminent danger. And it didn't just come out of people's mouths. It was written on their faces, and it hung in the air.

There was a lot of special typhoon talk, too—shrill words and flags with numbers that told your Humans what to do. "The flag's been hoisted" was heard everywhere— sometimes from Mr. Leung or from one Human to another outside our supermarket, other times from the man on TV, who would pace back and forth, waving his arms wildly in front of pictures of big black clouds. If the message came over the radio when my Mom and I were in our car, we'd head home as fast as we could so that she could call my Dad.

A No. 1 didn't seem to be a problem. Someone may have seen a typhoon, but even if they did, it might not come to Hong Kong. A No.

---

4 *tai feng*, a great wind, from *tu* = big + *feng* = wind

2 was on its way, though I don't think you had to go home that very second. But WHOA! Let me tell you, No. 3 to No. 10 were serious business, and when their flags went up, every Human in Hong Kong went home.

There was another warning I used to get that didn't have a number. It was one of those knowing feelings you get inside, except it was different from ones I'd had before when I'd heard a rustle in the bushes or a swish from a nearby tree. With this, there was nothing—no noise from any creature or insect, no whisper from the wind. The only sound was silence, and it was more frightening than anything I'd ever experienced. Our Humans call it "the calm before the storm." But when my Mom called out, "Harry...Come on...NOW!" in the shrill tone she saved especially for typhoons, the calm would disappear as quickly as it had set in.

There'd be a mad rush of people running into our supermarket, and it must have been helter-skelter inside, because in no time, they'd come flying back out, jump into their cars and squeal off. The wind would pick up, until swirls of dust were spinning past me and my eyes were stinging with tears, then the whole sky would dissolve into dark shades of gray. I could see flashes of lightning in the distance, cutting through the gloom and hear the thunder cracking overhead. And all the time, I'd be waiting outside the door for my Mom, peering through the window to see if I could spot her in the frenzy and willing her to hurry so that we could get home before it was too late.

By the time she came out, great black clouds would be looming overhead, and we'd race them down the hill, trying to outrun them so that we'd be safely inside before they unleashed their fury. My Dad was always there ahead of us, putting enormous strips of white tape in big Xs across our front windows in case they smashed in with the force of the wind and the rain. Sometimes, we'd watch from the verandah and as the winds whistled and howled past, we'd see swarms of tiny birds darting back and forth and swooping erratically, searching for a safe haven somewhere in the trees. The rain would begin falling—gently at first, then heavily, hammering down angrily on our roof for hours on end. Lightning would illuminate the huge waves rolling toward the shore, and when they hit, they'd crash against the rocks, sending a towering wall of water shooting high up into the air.

As soon as the thunder began cracking directly above us, I'd head for cover in my bathroom, where I'd cower in a corner for hours. The rain would lash against the windows, and my Mom and Dad would come and comfort me, knowing I was too scared to do anything but just lie there. When my own force of nature called, they'd take me outside and point to a spot right in front of the door, which was fine with me, seeing as all I wanted to do was get it over with so I could go back inside and not be blown to the Outer Limits.

Something very weird about typhoons is that they have Human and/or dawg names. I don't know if there's ever been a Typhoon Harry—if there was, it wasn't when we lived in Hong Kong—but we did have a Kent, and when he came slamming through, all hell broke loose. He was the biggest typhoon Hong Kong had seen in a long time; in fact, he was so big that one of those "If I hadn't seen and experienced all that I have firsthand, I don't think I'd believe it myself" things happened under his roving eye, if you get my drift. You can take it or leave it, but I saw it with my own two, and so did my Mom and Dad.

It was still light and we were watching the storm from our living room window. The wind was getting stronger by the minute, churning and howling and sweeping the rain along with it, when we saw what looked like a black-and-silver shadow moving above the trees that banked down the hill in front of our flat. It was gathering speed as it went, rolling and skipping and tumbling all over itself.

Suddenly, it was close enough for us to make out what it was, and as it flew by, my Mom and Dad stood there with their mouths gaped open in blank astonishment, as if they'd seen a ghost for the very first time. When they finally managed to speak, the words came stumbling out in a muddled array of confusion. "Th....a.........th....at.....wa..... uh....zz...was......an....A...........IR.........an...AI.....IR...CON... DI-DI....SH...SHON....ER," they gasped, staring at each other in shock and disbelief. And that's exactly what it was—a flying air conditioner, zooming right past our flat in Chung Hom Kok! Kent was a No. 9 on the scale, which my Dad says "is as high as you want to go, thank you very much."

Most typhoons lasted for two or three days and afterward the sky would be wide and crystal blue, with frothy white clouds and the sea shimmering silver in the sunlight. When I'd step outside for the first time, I'd take an enormous breath and feel a rush of squeaky-clean air filling my lungs, and I couldn't wait to run on the beach.

The wind and rain would leave their devastation everywhere, soaking the hills and valleys, turning streams into raging rivers and bringing mud and twisted debris sliding down the mountainsides. One day, a humungous uprooted tree blocked the road to Tai Tam, the country park where I ran with my Mom most mornings, so that nothing could pass, but the next day it was business as usual.

* * *

My Humans are always telling their friends that "most people think Hong Kong's just a blah…blah…blah jungle (?!!?) of flats with the harbor (?!!?) and boats in between" and that's because they've never been to the country parks or the grassy hills and wild places, with their steep slopes sweeping down into valleys and their trails winding through woodlands to the red-earth shores of the reservoirs below. These are some of my best memories of Hong Kong.

When my Dad was home, we'd take long walks through the lush tropical forests up beyond the reservoirs, starting out early to catch the light of the morning dew glistening on giant spider webs and bouncing off bright red and yellow flowers that hung from vines and looked like birds. Before we reached the trail that led across the top and down to the water, we'd stop for lunch at a nice shady spot under a canopy of green. While my Mom and Dad sat on a moss-covered log and ate their sandwiches, I'd scour the underbrush for a stick to take home—not just any old stick, a perfect stick, the kind with mottled bark that you can chew on forever without getting bored.

After lunch, the breeze would fall off, and by the time we crossed the bridge, the water below would be flat calm, without a single ripple, like a mirror of blue ice reflecting the green hills and wispy clouds float-ing past them. When we reached the water's edge, I'd brace myself before I ran in then do a double take upon seeing another Harry that looked exactly like me. But in the next breath, I'd be charging in to swim with him.

Sometimes, I'd go hiking with just my Mom up the Wilson Trail, which went higher than most, with amazing views of peaks and wooded valleys, silvery seas and white sandy beaches stretching out for miles below. When we were at the top one after-noon, and she was "way out there" in that faraway place your Humans (especially Moms) sometimes go, she looked at me with complete confidence that I'd understand every word she was about to say. "Do you know, Hars," she said, "I think heaven's knowing what to look for in simple things like the mountains and the sea" (?!!?). Then she hugged me, and I was spinning with joy over how much my Humans love me.

On our way down that day, we saw a bamboo snake (AKA pit viper) on the trail. He was a master of camouflage, with bright green and yellow markings on his back, just like the bamboo that grows all over Hong Kong; in fact, if he hadn't slithered right across my paw, I would have thought that's all he was.

Aside from snakes, Brie and I have had about twenty-seven million "live" encounters with insects like the wingless litter cockroach, rats and mice, birds, chickens, roosters, Brahma bulls, water buffalo, lizards, elephants and sun bears, to name a few, and trust me, running into some of these creatures is about as far as you can get from meeting Griffey and your other VBCFs at the Dawg Park in Vancouver. My Humans have come up with different names for these encounters, depending on how serious they are, and because we're usually with our Mom when they happen, she puts them in the proper file.

If whatever happened was completely over the top, my Dad will be told as soon as he walks in the door that "We had a situation today." Then they'll sit down and discuss it with very serious expressions on their faces and no-nonsense tones in their voices.

Incidents, which happen more frequently, aren't nearly as urgent and can usually wait until they're having a drink of something or eating dinner. Halfway through my Mom's recounting, they're both laughing so hard they're almost choking, and as soon as she's finished, she tells the same story all over again, causing further hysterics.

Emergencies are a separate category altogether, and even though they can result from a "live" encounter, they can also result from an accident or just plain old bad luck. Response to these must be immediate, with a call to my Dad and a mad taxi ride to the vet. Between Brie and me, we've already had three, which tells you unequivocally that our lives as expat canines aren't exactly a mellow meander down the Mekong!

The first was mine, after I drank some bad water from the field across from our house in Hanoi, except my Mom and Dad didn't call it bad water; they called it "a hazardous material," which I figure is on a totally different level! The second was when Brie hurt her foot in West Lake in Hanoi and had to be rushed to Dr. Die at the university. And the third was my run-in with a Rottweiler. My Dad describes that one as "a combative situation." You'll hear the Dawg-awful details of all of these when I get to the right place in my tales. But for now, we're still in Hong Kong and I have yet to introduce you to my second VBCF in the whole world—ARCEA, New York City dawg.

I never dreamed I'd have another VBCF like Griffey until I met ARCEA (his Mom and Dad write it ARCEA but say it *same same* 'RCA') and discovered all VBCFs are a little different. My Mom and I had just come back from a run in Tai Tam and there, coming out of the flat next door, fresh off the plane from New York City, was ARCEA with his Humans, Suzy and Dung.

Like Griffey and me, ARCEA had a namesake, but it wasn't sports related; it had to do with "retro" (?!!?). According to my Mom and Dad, retro refers to things from "bygone days that have come back again." You wouldn't think it needed much clarification other than "Buh-bye, gone, and I'm back," except I think it gets more complicated than that when Humans become obsessed with it. It sounds a lot like Captain Crunch's airplane memorabilia if you ask me.

Anyway, ARCEA's namesake was this well-known retro advertising dawg who was the logo for the RCA record company, one of the oldest record companies in the United States of America. He was known as His Master's Voice, or HMV for short, and was seen on billboards and TV all over the world staring in bewilderment into a talking machine. I think he could hear his Human's voice inside. ARCEA didn't look anything like him; he was a Golden just like me. But his Mom and Dad obviously loved retro and that's how he got his name. I was a little

envious at first because ARCEA sounded much more glamorous than Harry Cleveland Brown Howard, but when I thought about how much my Dad loves "those Browns," it didn't bother me anymore.

The main difference between ARCEA and me was our coats. Mine was Golden and ARCEA's was a sleek, shiny red. He was also much thinner with longer legs, and he could run like the wind. I don't know why, but ARCEA wasn't nearly as crazy about food as I am. My Dad says I'm "obsessed with eating," and he even told Big Joe that I "don't distinguish between filet mignon and tennis balls," which isn't entirely true.

When they first arrived in Hong Kong, ARCEA and his Humans had a lot of acclimatizing and unpacking to do, so two or three days passed before we spent quality time together. Our first official outing was with our Moms down the trail in front of our flats. A few sniffs in the right places, then instant wiggling and wagging, as if we'd known each other in another life, and we were off like bullets, dekeing in and out of the bushes and jumping over fallen branches and narrow streams until the path ended, giving way to a stretch of sandy beach and the South China Sea. When ARCEA bounded into the water, I was right behind him, and by the time our Moms got there, we were miles down the beach, jumping in and out of the surf then rolling in the sand.

It was ARCEA who put my fear of deep water to rest. He was fearless when it came to water; in fact, he was fearless about everything. I don't know if it was his New York upbringing or just ARCEA from the day he was born, but he was an all-round athlete, a teacher, a performer and a master prankster!

Most mornings, we'd go with Suzy and my Mom to the Tai Tam reservoirs. ARCEA and I would run on ahead, taking a shortcut through the woods down to the beach, while Suzy and my Mom yakked, guffawed, drank their coffee and took forever to get there. While we were

waiting for them, we'd dig our way to China in the red sand, spewing it everywhere, then scamper up over the rocks to the bluff and jump down into the water.

The first time ARCEA went in, I ran straight back to the beach, but the next time, he zoomed around in circles, luring me into a chase. When he charged up to the bluff, I was hot on his tail, and the second he took off, I flew in after him without the slightest hesitation. When I surfaced, he was right there waiting for me with a huge "Way to go, Harry" grin from ear to ear. As soon as our Moms arrived, we went through the whole sequence again to show them what he'd taught me.

In the late afternoons we'd meet for one last run around our parking lot, with Suzy and my Mom egging us on. ARCEA would start out by hiding in one spot and keep on moving. All I'd see would be a red blur zooming around a corner, then he'd disappear. But even ARCEA, top-notch athlete, couldn't keep it up forever. Eventually, I'd catch him and we'd wrestle each other to the ground. Panting and deliriously happy, we'd flop over on our stomachs and lie there like brothers in arms.

The day ARCEA left for good, I waited outside his door until it was almost time for the sun to drop into the sea, watching the long afternoon shadows moving across the pavement where his car was usually parked and thinking about our sunset run. But he never came back, and after a while my Mom came and took me home. I lay on the sofa with my head in her lap for the rest of the night, while she rubbed my tummy and talked to me in a very quiet voice. She told me it was "hard being an expat—for us, too, Har," because "friends like ARCEA, Suzy and Dung are here one day and gone the next."

When I went over the next morning to see if ARCEA really had gone, the door was open, but there was nothing there. I caught a little of his scent, but it was almost completely overpowered by moving smells. I felt lonely for the longest time after ARCEA, Suzy and Dung went back to New York; in fact, Hong Kong was never the same for me.

We still keep in touch with Suzy. Recently, she wrote that ARCEA had put on five pounds and "there was a new sheriff in town, cutting out table scraps for his own good." My Mom says the same thing to me when she gives me a smaller portion than Brie, which is most of the time.

On Fridays they have Casual Day in New York and ARCEA goes to Suzy's office in Greenwich Village. He gets to follow her to the photocopy machine, then lounge under her desk until it's time to go home. Not long ago, my Mom and Dad spent a day in New York and ARCEA was even allowed to go into a boutique called Morgan Le Fay and sit under the table at a fancy dawg-friendly restaurant in SoHo where they ate lunch all afternoon.

Sometimes I dream about living in New York. Brie and I aren't allowed in any restaurants in Ho Chi Minh City. My Mom says it would be "utter pandemonium," with Brie chasing the chickens and me going for *phở*, which is almost the same as Mr. Leung's Shanghai noodles except it's Vietnamese. Also, they don't have dawg-friendly restaurants in Vietnam like they do in New York and lots of other places, because there's a different meaning to dawg-friendly— as in dawg-unfriendly for us and dawg-on-the-menu-friendly for Vietnamese Humans!

Something else happened around the same time as ARCEA left Hong Kong. It was Chibi. I think he was getting pretty old for a cat. I don't really know how old that is, but he wasn't doing much of anything other than sleeping. He didn't even come over and badger me anymore. When I woke up one morning, he was taking slow, rattled breaths, and my Mom bundled him up in a blanket and took him off in the car. He didn't come home that night; in fact, that was the last time I ever saw Chibi. I decided he'd gone to sleep forever, like the orange cat that used to live near ARCEA's flat, but then one day when my Mom was talking to me she said, "Cats have nine lives." After that, I didn't feel as sad for Chibi, because I know he's living all of his lives as an expat in some far-off mystical land like Egypt, where he probably came from in the first place. I still miss Chibi a lot. He was the only feline friend I've ever had and one awesome cat.

* * *

Besides my Mom and Dad, Mr. Leung, ARCEA, and Suzy and Dung, I had one other very close Human friend in Hong Kong, who used to take me way up into the hills and wild places. He lived in our building and his name was Mr. Ian. It's a mystery to me how Humans always know what day it is, seeing as they all seem pretty much the same to me, but whenever Mr. Ian knocked on the door to ask if he could "borrow wee Harry to get lost in Tai Tam," I knew it was Saturday. Mr. Ian came from Scotland, and my Mom says Scottish people always say "wee this and wee that," which is why Mr. Ian called me "wee Harry," even though I wasn't so wee anymore.

The closest I ever came to actually getting lost in the hills was when Mr. Ian would suddenly disappear off the trail and vanish into thin air. Worried that he'd gone on without me, I'd charge on ahead, then stop dead in my tracks, figuring he was up to his old tricks. When I'd run back to find him, he'd suddenly leap out from behind a tree with a loud "Gotcha, Harry" and an enormous grin. I loved Mr. Ian, and I loved all my Saturdays with him—all except for one. It was the day we crossed the Bridge of No Return, the day I learned how terrifying it is to be completely and utterly paralyzed by fear.

The day began like any other, hiking high up into the hills, running along the catch waters, dodging twigs and branches and butterflies, and feeling the brush of the light breeze against our faces. Every so often, I'd stop for a swim in one of the reservoirs, and Mr. Ian would throw sticks for me to fetch, then call out in his boisterous voice, "Come on, Harry, my mate," and we'd be on our way again.

It was well after lunchtime when we reached the top that afternoon, so I knew we'd gone higher than usual. The temperature had fallen off sharply, and I could feel ice-cold air settling in around me. As we rounded the next curve and the bridge came into view, my tummy did one of those flip-flops that come with the first inklings of fear, and before I'd taken my next breath, my nerves had worked their way through my entire body.

The bridge was shrouded in a ghostly gray mist from the water cascading beneath it and was by far the narrowest bridge I'd seen in all my walks through Hong Kong. There was something terribly foreboding about it, the way it was suspended there, high above the raging rock pools below, with nothing in between except an icy haze. But there was something else, something that made my blood turn cold and my heart skip a beat. It had no railings.

Mr. Ian went first, thinking I was right behind him, but I'd stopped to try to calm my nerves and steady my shaking limbs before I started across. Finally, I began to move forward ever so slowly, placing one foot in front of the other and inching my way along like a crab on a tightrope, keeping my body tilted to one side as I went, because everything was out of kilter and I felt better leaning slightly to one side. But after I'd taken only a few short steps, a cool gust of wind hit me from behind and I immediately froze, too terrified to move a single muscle.

All I wanted to do was close my eyes to block out the terrible emptiness, but I knew if I did, it would send my head into a spin and I'd plunge to the rocks and raging waters below. I needed something, anything to keep me from falling, but there was nothing. So I did the only thing I could. I stayed exactly where I was, with my paws rooted to the slippery surface beneath me and my eyes fixed on a tree on the far side to try to keep my balance. In the distance, I could hear Mr. Ian's voice coaxing me, telling me it was all right, but no matter how many times he called out or how soothing his voice sounded, I couldn't muster up the courage to move a single step. I could feel the ice-cold spray against my face and hear the water rushing and roaring beneath me. My legs had turned to jelly, and I had to concentrate as hard as I could to tighten my muscles so that they wouldn't give way completely and send me hurtling over the edge to a certain death. It felt as though I stood there forever, every second an eternity.

Suddenly, out of the very corner of my eye, I saw Mr. Ian shuffling sideways along the slippery planks, making his way back to the spot where I stood, speaking softly all the time until he was right there beside me, one hand under my chin, looking me straight in the eye like my Mom and Dad do. "It's okay, Harry," he said. "You're going to have to trust me on this one. We're going to do it together—you and I—slow and steady, one step at a time."

And so Mr. Ian and I crossed that Bridge of No Return together, just like he said we would. And when we reached the other side, I was so happy to be on solid ground, I felt tears running down my cheeks as he rubbed my ears and scrunched the fur behind my neck. He told my Mom and Dad I won a Boy Scout medal that day, but all I remember is how good it felt to have someone you trust right there beside you, every step of the way. My Mom says it's like "holding hands when you walk around a dark corner," which is exactly how it felt.

Not long after, Mr. Ian moved to China and we moved to Lantau Island, which we got to by ferry from Hong Kong. The boatman made my Mom put a muzzle on me, and I remember feeling embarrassed, even though I didn't know anyone on the boat.

I think it's possible to feel embarrassed all by yourself, and it's usually when you have to do something that makes you look or feel "ri-dic-ru-lous," like wearing one of those plastic lampshades on your head after you've been to Dr. Die and bumping into all the furniture. The absolute worst was when I had to wear a cone after I'd had a procedure in a spot I'd rather not discuss and was managing to twist around and gnaw at it. If you can believe it, my Mom and Dad put me in my Dad's shorts with suspenders so that I wouldn't irritate it any more than I already had. All I wanted to do was become invisible.

After I had the muzzle on, we went to the upper deck, and as I sat gazing up at my Mom with those mournful eyes that usually get me off the hook, she put her hand under my chin and said, "I know, Hars, it's really stupid," then took it off. Sitting up on that top deck with my Mom, feeling the mist on my face and the changing winds, was another of my very best things in Hong Kong.

Sometimes we'd go on a different boat to another island called Peng Chau so that my Mom could go shopping at the wet market[5] (?!!?). I had to wait outside with my Dad, because of the likelihood of a full-scale riot if I went in, but we could see her moving through the slippery aisles filled with fruit and vegetables, fish and buckets of sloppy entrails from the dead things hanging on hooks above the long, wooden tables. When Big Joe came to visit all the way from Canada, he came with us to Peng Chau one day and almost keeled over when a singsongy voice rang out loud and clear from inside the market. "Rei

---

5 Common in Asia, the name comes from the extensive use of water to wash down the floors and keep the fruits and vegetables fresh and the fish alive.

ho, HaLLy!" We turned around to see a
hand waving madly above all the heads
and Mr. Leung, my very best Hong Kong
friend, running toward us with his smiling
eyes and gold-toothed grin. Big Joe never
got over the fact that a Chinese Human
on Peng Chau knew me. "Harry," he said
with a chuckle, "you've made more friends
in more places than most people do in a
lifetime." I guess Big Joe knew that making
VBFs was my number two mission in life.

My Mom told everyone that Lantau
reminded her of Ireland, because it was wild and rugged, with grassy
hills and trails that wound their way up to awesome peaks. The
mountains ran like a dragon's back along the top, and once we got
up there, there were hardly any trees. In the summer, when the black
clouds loomed overhead and the rains swept in, the hills would turn
a deep emerald green. We could walk for an entire afternoon without
meeting a single soul, and on the way down, we'd follow the clear
mountain streams, jumping from one rock to another, and I'd swim
in the deep pools with my Mom, which was one of the coolest things
I've ever done.

* * *

Suddenly, it seemed as if everyone was on the move. It was June 30,
1997, and the only thing on my Mom and Dad's minds was "Hong
Kong going back to China." That night, they went out to watch "history in the making" (?!!?) from a junk in the harbor.

You may not know this, but there are two kinds of junk: the special
Chinese boat a lot of Humans watched the fireworks from that night
and the other junk people throw into Victoria Harbor all the time,
like refrigerators and computers. Anyway, after all the flurry and fuss
about Hong Kong leaving, my Mom and Dad were up at the crack of

dawn the next morning to watch the Chinese army march into Hong Kong. It didn't appear that Hong Kong had gone anywhere.

When my kennel appeared in the kitchen and my Mom started crawling inside to coax me in for breakfast (it's amazing what your Humans will do!), I knew we were leaving, too, and that my own marching orders would be coming down any day.

Now, at this point in my life, I'd pretty much decided that fear comes from the unknown rather than the known; in other words, if you've done something once, you should be okay with it the next time. But the truth was, I wasn't. I could feel that same queasiness creeping into my tummy as I was being rolled onto the plane, and strangely enough, it was the knowing what was ahead that pushed my nerves from my stomach to my limbs, then all the way up to my neck. There was a lesson to be learned from this. If Dawg had wanted Goldens to fly, he would have given us wings, not just feathers!

Takeoff was as terrifying as I remembered, with the same rumbling vibrations and sluggish climb to the top, with a full load of fuel and cargo and all the Humans lounging around on the upper deck. Thankfully, once we reached the magic Outer Limits mark, I was able to slide into a pretty good Stage 4 of my snooze cycle that lasted until the jolt just before our descent.

CHAPTER 4
Home

I vaguely remembered a thought floating around in my head just before takeoff, but it got lost somewhere in the underside of that 747 and didn't pop up again until we were back on terra firma. Then, BOINK! There it was, front and center of my brain. I was disappointed in myself. I knew my Mom and I were going to Hong Kong when we left Vancouver, but I had no idea where we were going when we left Hong Kong, and we were already on the ground. I don't know how I missed it, but luckily I didn't have to wait long to find out. As soon as I came out into the oversized baggage area, which is a little insulting when you think about it, and heard the joyful sound of my sister Sara's voice, I knew we were home, and my heart was as full as it could be.

Now, home can be a little confusing for returning expats, canine or otherwise, for the simple reason that you've just left a place you've been calling "home" for quite some time and arrived at another with the same name. But it doesn't take long before you realize that this one is different. It's not just where your Humans are and your leash is hung; it's a lot more. It's where you came from in the beginning and where you go back to when you need the comfort of real friends and family, not just ones who come and go. When you get there after being

away for a long time, you might think it's changed, but you soon discover it hasn't, and you feel all warm and tingly inside knowing it's the same as it always was.

A lot of my Mom and Dad's friends called me by name, and whenever they said "Harry," it was warm and welcoming and I knew they were genuinely happy to see me. They told me I'd grown into a very handsome boy, which I hadn't really thought about, though my paws had long since stopped giving me grief. Almost all my Mom and Dad's time with their friends was spent laughing and telling stories, and even though a lot of them sounded the same to me, it didn't seem to matter to them. They told them over and over and laughed harder every time. And it was the best kind of laughter I'd ever heard. It was the laughter of old friends and it came from deep inside and flowed through my entire being.

Soon after we came back, we drove to meet Griffey, Max and Riley at our *same same* place at Pacific Spirit Park and we were instantly VBFs again—sniffing, wagging and wiggling our behinds in excited recognition. The moment our leads were unclipped, we were off, chasing each other through the trees, jumping and scampering over logs and barking as loud as we could at the squeaky-clean air. Every so often, we'd circle back to make sure our Moms and Dads weren't lost, before charging off again.

Some mornings, everything would be unusually still, and I'd wish as hard as I could that what I thought had happened really and truly had. I'd run to the window, and sure enough, there'd be a blanket of pure white snow covering the ground and icy crystals glistening on the big trees in our backyard. I didn't know there was a special smell to snow, but when I took my first deep breath after stepping outside, I discovered there is. My Mom calls it "Harry's Sense of Snow."

Of course, there were things that were new and different, which you have to expect when you've been away for a long time. One was our new yellow car that my Humans called LL after my Mom's lemon loaf. When we went for rides, I'd get to sit up front, and the best thing of all was the top came down, so on sunny days you could go everywhere with the fresh air brushing against your muzzle and your ears flapping in the breeze. I could ride around in Lemon Loaf all day long without getting bored!

There were new places, too—one where we'd go running in the mornings and sometimes for walks after dinner. It was called the Flats, which sounds almost like our house in Hong Kong, but there was no resemblance. These flats were near a river and had country roads lined with bushes that were heavy with blackberries in the summer. There were horses in fields, with sleek black or brown coats, long, thin legs and beautiful dark, shining eyes. When the weather got warmer, they stood in one place with their heads bowed eating grass, and sometimes they'd walk around in circles with a Human on their back. I loved their smell, and filed it away in my database, along with all the other new scents I came across. Some of my favorites were freshly cut grass and flowers blooming in the spring, piles of dark soil sitting by the side of the road and hay stacked against wooden fences. But there was another smell that came into its own soon after we got back to Canada that my Humans just couldn't seem to come to grips with. It's called "putrid," and to this day, it's one of the best discoveries of my life. According to our Humans, it's "anything that's decayed (a state of disgusting disintegration), rancid (a state of reek-ing remains) or dead (not so dearly departed)."

I'd gotten into it a few times in Hong Kong, when I was hiking or running along the beaches on Lantau, but my Mom and Dad dis-missed it as puppy dawg antics, which are more or less acceptable when you're one or two years old. It wasn't until I got back to Canada that I became totally "obsessed with it." My sister, Sara, says "it's a guy thing," and she's probably right, because I've only seen Brie go for it once or twice, and I think she was just copying me, like she does.

Anyway, if it happens to be your thing and it was definitely mine, it will surface as soon as you pick up the tiniest whiff, and the second you do, your instinct will kick in. From that moment on, everything that happens is completely beyond your control!

Your Mom sees the subtle twitch of your nose as the foul scent dances lightly by on a breath of air and notices your stance has changed from ree-laxed to full alert, ready for takeoff. You hear her desperate cry, "Puh-leeze, Harry…Noooo…" But her words are carried away with the wind, because that power inside has taken hold, and there is nothing on the face of the earth that can stop you now. In fact, you're already long gone, tearing through the trees or marshes at a million miles per hour, heading directly for the spot for today's roll-in.

When you get there, you go directly to ground, pivoting slightly as you ease yourself down into the muck so that one side of your head and your ear are the first parts of your body to writhe in your discovery. And writhe you do, with full-body twists and turns, pressing every single muscle of your back, shoulders and neck into the grunge as deeply as you can. The moment you make contact, this incredible feeling of euphoria sweeps over you, elevating you to a state of ecstasy you've never come close to before.

The first time it happened to me, I thought it must be a rite of passage, like some of Brie's cavorts and crazy puppy chews, but when I didn't outgrow it, I knew it was something much deeper, like a secret ritual among certain boy dawgs. We don't talk about it. There's no need to, because there's a special "knowing" that's inherently understood among us from the day we're born.

When you're done, which is no more than a minute or two max, you bound back to your Mom, wagging your tail ecstatically and grinning so hard the corners of your mouth are stretched all the way to your ears, completely oblivious to the fact that she's not looking at you with her usual admiration and awe. You wait patiently while she snaps your leash onto your collar and then set off for home. The only thing you really care about as you bounce along beside her is that you're one happy puppy, though it does dawn on you about halfway that the only words she's spoken since the incident are "Why, Harry… Why?" in a voice close to tears, pleading for an answer. More than anything, you wish you could shout it out at the top of your lungs—"Why not?"—then explain it to her. But you can't, and she wouldn't get it anyway. You take a long, deep breath in, shake your head sadly and resign yourself to the fact that there are countless things about dawgs that our Humans will never come close to understanding.

As soon as you walk in the gate, she ties your leash to a tree at the side of the driveway and storms into the garage. A minute later, she reappears, armed with herbal shampoo in one hand and a high-powered hose in the other, and proceeds to give you the most rigorous scrub imaginable—soaping, lathering, kneading and scouring every furrow and fold of your body, making absolutely sure that not even the tiniest crease or crevice is left uncleansed. You gaze up at her lovingly as she rubs you down with a fluffy white towel.

By the time she's finished, there's not a microscopic hair that could produce DNA evidence of the very best thing that's happened to you that week, possibly that month, and the only thing left for you to do is file the memory of it away in that compartment of your brain labeled "Almost Heaven," sub-file "Putrid," sub-sub-file, "Grunge I Have Come to Know and Love," and bring it out whenever the spirit moves you. Something I find a little strange is that sometimes when she's going on about Brie and me, like she tends to do, with that "Love me, love my dogs" song in her heart, I hear her laughing about this very subject, then adding, "Harry isn't terribly selective—*nước mắm* (Vietnamese fish sauce), dead fish, rats, durian, pretty much any putrid will do." I don't understand the inconsistency, because when we run home together after a particularly good roll-in, she immediately lapses into silence, barely speaking to me. I put it down to her being lost in thought, which is where Humans often go.

Anyway, when I think about everything that happened the year we were back in Canada, there's one day that stands out far above the rest. It was the day we brought my little sister home, a day that changed my life forever.

CHAPTER 5
Brie

My Mom and Dad used to take me to a pet store in Vancouver called Star Pets, where we got to know the owner, Louisa. She was "*très* French," according to my Dad, and had a lilt to her voice that reminded me of Mr. Ian's, only a wee bit softer. Every time we visited her, she'd scratch behind my ears and say, "*Oooooh là là,* Harr-eee," and the words would roll off her tongue like butter. Her eyes never stopped smiling, and when she laughed, they laughed with her.

She had a beautiful Black Lab named Shadow, who would sit quietly at her feet, preening, except when he was out on one of his runs with his Dad, Maurice, who was also "*très* French," according to my Mom. Shadow's coat was shiny and black as coal, and I thought it must be something to see him running on the beach with Maurice, racing to the rhythm of the wind.

Anyway, not long before we left Canada for Vietnam, my Dad got a call from Louisa. Right after he put the phone down, I heard the word "puppy," and so began the story of Brie. It has a heart-rending beginning.

A friend of Louisa's came home after a holiday and found a little Golden running back and forth between her garden and her neighbors' in a frenzy. Two weeks before, they'd gone back to Hong Kong for the summer and, to her horror, had left this poor little creature chained in their back garden by herself. Someone had been pushing food and water through the fence, but she was underfed, dehydrated, frightened to death and crazy in confinement. She'd somehow managed to chew through the links of her chain and had been jumping the fence and running frantically between the two houses ever since. When Louisa's friend found her, she took her to a shelter, then called Louisa to see if she knew anyone who would take her permanently, which is where my Mom and Dad came in. Of course, all of this was unknown to me the day they told me we were going for a car ride with Big Joe. So on that beautiful spring afternoon when we set out for what I thought was going to be a long walk along the river, I had no idea what was in store for me or that it would change my life forever.

Instead of going the way we usually did, we crossed a bridge and turned onto a narrow dirt road. My Dad drove slowly, and when we came to a small white house at the end, he turned into the driveway. Big Joe and I waited in the car, and my Mom and Dad disappeared inside. I remember all kinds of barking coming from the house, and when I looked at the front window, I could see wide-eyed little faces peeking out from behind the curtains—a lot of them!

The front door finally opened, and my Mom and Dad came out with a lady I'd never seen before. To my complete and utter surprise, bouncing and jumping wildly between them was the scrawniest Golden puppy I'd ever seen. When I looked closely, I could see it wasn't really a "puppy" puppy, because it was long-legged like ARCEA, but it was skinnier than skinny and totally out of control. My Dad had a very serious look on his face and was using all the strength he possessed to try and get it to stay down. They were heading directly for the car, and my instinct told me right off the bat that the whole thing spelled trouble—big trouble.

Later, I heard my Dad say it was "out of character for Harry" and my Mom reply, "It was bound to happen—it was territorial" (?!!?), which could have meant anything. Having said that, there was one thing that was absolutely clear to me during those first few minutes when she made her grand entrance into my life, tumbling into the back seat and falling all over me, and it was that she was in "my" car, in "my" corner of the back seat, wearing "my" red leash. And the minute those thoughts went through my head, something started seething inside me and a strange gravelly sound came gurgling up from the bottom of my throat, a sound I'd only heard once before, from those poor dawgs in confinement at Pok Fu Lam, so you can imagine the shock that ran through me when I realized that exact same noise was coming from me, harry@harry.calm.

I'd growled for the first time in my life, and the more I GRRrowled, the more she jumped on me, until I couldn't stand it for one more second. So right there in the back seat, I went at her. And for the next few minutes, we were just one huge mass of tangled Golden fur, with me snarling, growling, kicking and biting that poor little puppy; Big Joe and my Mom looking on in horror; and my Dad doing his best to drive the car.

Suddenly, he turned his head and hollered at the very top of his lungs: "STOP, HARRY, STOP! RIGHT THIS INSTANT! LEAVE HER ALONE." The anger in his voice cut through the air like a knife and in a flash, it was over, as quickly as it had started. We drove the rest of the way home in silence—me with my head between my paws, feeling shame, and my Mom beside me with the puppy's head in her lap, stroking her gently and giving me an occasional forgiving pat. When we reached our street, there was some hushed conversation between my Mom and Dad and Big Joe, and as we turned into the driveway, I heard my Mom say, "It's all right, little Brie, you're safe now. You don't have to be afraid anymore. We're home." I knew then that they'd named her Brie.

That night, when I was curled up near my Mom on the sofa, still feeling shame, and my Dad was sitting on the floor with Brie's head draped over his leg, rubbing her ears, I heard the same words I'd heard in the car: "You're safe, little Brie," and I knew she was. I felt a rush of warmth knowing she had a real family and a place to call home and that my Mom and Dad would take her for runs and swims and car rides, throw balls for her, lay her blanket out at night and snuggle her in after a particularly exhausting day, just like they'd done for me ever since I was a puppy. She was already returning their affection in spades, wagging at her name and practically everything they said, pulling the threads on my Dad's socks and jumping up to lick his face, nudge his ear and chew on his collar. It was love at first sight, and if she'd been able to speak, she would have told them herself. But she didn't have to. They already knew.

The next day, they took her to the vet to have some stitches taken out where she'd been "fixed." I had no idea what she'd had fixed, but I knew one thing that needed fixing right away, and it was the way she was. In your wildest dreams, you can't imagine the pandemonium that broke out in our house after Brie came home. She never walked; in fact, I wondered if she even knew how. Every day was a series of wild bursts of energy spent tearing through the house from top to bottom, sliding around the corners, skidding across the floors, banging off the walls and leaping up and down off the beds. But no matter how hard she landed, it never bothered her. In fact, nothing bothered her.

If there was a Human within range, she'd jump up against their chest with full force so that she could lick their neck and face, then nip at their fingers. My Mom would stand there watching with a dreamy smile on her face, then say to the Human trying to pick themselves up off the floor and regain their composure, "Don't you just love her? She's so affectionate." Nicknames began inserting themselves into my Humans' vocabulary that were soft and loving, like "little girl" and "little princess." Her blithe, breezy spirit and infinite curiosity about everything around her had an amazing effect on everyone she met. There was something so spontaneous and joyful inside her, along with an unwavering trust and innocence that stayed with her throughout her life. When she'd lift her head up and gaze at you with her beautiful coffee-colored eyes, her whole face would light up, and then she'd break into an enormous grin from ear to ear.

One day, my Mom left the kitchen to get something, and when she came back, Brie was standing on her hind legs against the counter with her head cocked to one side and three-quarters of a freshly baked lemon loaf in her mouth. "It's delicious," her eyes were saying. "Thank you so much for making it for me." My Mom and Dad never reprimanded her for anything. They were too far gone!

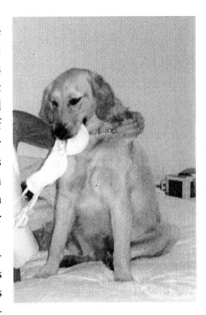

Bras were her favorite non-edible chews and running shoes a close second. When she was caught red-handed with a brand-new pair of Nikes, she just sat there, staring up at my Mom as if to say:

Nike Air,
I know … it's not fair.
But what could I do?
They smelled like you.

I never liked it when my Dad lifted me up on my hind legs, but Brie loved it from the very beginning and can stay there forever, especially when she's on gecko patrol, which was every night after my Dad came home from work in Vietnam. As soon as she spots her prey, she stands absolutely still, contemplating her plan of attack, then props herself up against the wall and skitters back and forth to get into position. When she's exactly where she wants to be, she springs straight up into the air, grabs the gecko by the tail and brings him down, separating his tail from the rest of his body. Having accomplished her goal, she watches in total astonishment as the tail continues to wiggle on the floor and the head and torso scuttle off in the opposite direction.

She took to the outdoors immediately, flying around the garden in circles, trampling flower beds and breaking off branches she'd chew to mulch and leave in scattered bits across the lawn. And every single afternoon, after I'd just settled into one of my favorite snoozing spots well out of sight, her radar would click in and she'd appear out of nowhere, running at top speed before launching herself into the air, splaying her legs and coming down right on top of me. But no matter how much she annoyed me or how many times she stole my toys or dug up tennis balls I'd spent the entire morning burying, I knew I had to grin and bear it because if I so much as raised a paw, I'd hear my Dad's angry voice and have to walk the Street of Shame, where I never wanted to go again.

After she'd been home for a while, she began tempting me to play, running toward me, then pausing to arch her back and stretch her legs before plunking herself down in front of me.

"Come on, Harry," her eyes would plead. "Puh-leeze, come and play with me!"

I resisted at first but finally gave in, which is what you end up doing when someone constantly badgers you and you run out of patience. We'd start out wrestling on our hind legs, biting each other's ears and making *hrrumm, hrrumm* sounds in our throats until one of us would get the upper paw and bring us both to ground, where we'd roll on

the grass until we were exhausted, just like I used to do with ARCEA. After the first round, we'd lie side by side, panting and listening to the sound of our breath, then suddenly jump up and start chasing each other around the garden at a zillion hundred miles an hour, flying in and out of the trees and bushes, leaving a cloud of dust in our wake.

After two or three laps, we'd come to a screeching halt and stare each other down for as long as it took for one of us to make the next move. Then we'd zoom off in the other direction, and the whole thing would start all over again. Even though we hadn't lived under the same roof, ARCEA had been like a brother to me, and now I had a real little sister in Brie. I think having a brother or sister is one of those things you don't miss until you have it, but once you do, you can't imagine your life without it.

* * *

There were whispers in the wind that we were moving, but I figured that was probably all they were, because life went on as usual, with only one exception. To my complete horror, our Mom and Dad had signed us up for a puppy class! I had ZEE-RO interest, but my Humans, with their tendency to underplay things, felt "Brie needed to calm down a little" (a little?) and didn't want me to feel left out. My Dad called it "an outing," which generally involved a car ride. That I could cope with. It was the puppy element that was hard to swallow, though surprisingly enough, once I got there, I didn't mind it nearly as much as I thought I would, which can happen when you're expecting the worst.

First, the teacher wasn't as bossy as the British lady with the shelf. I mean, she could be a little belittling at times, but I didn't quiver in my paws at the sound of her voice, and neither did my Mom and Dad. Second, almost everything we did was part of my daily routine, so I had most of it "down pat" before we even started. Take walking around in circles ad nauseam and staying glued to the teacher's side while she said "Heel." Like all Goldens, I mastered this as soon as I discovered it's what we have to do every day of our lives when we're on our quests to make NVBFs. So when she gave the command to heel, I did exactly what I've done with everyone else I've formed life-long friendships with. I positioned myself right beside her, nuzzled up against her hip and gazed into her eyes with the most forlorn expression I could come up with.

The problem was, she kept telling me to stop staring at her, insisting I was losing concentration. This was a total switch from all the other Humans I've tried this on, who immediately start scratching my ears and patting my head, without even realizing they're doing it, then call out in astonishment to their friend across the street, "Heh, Bill, would you look at this?"

Big Joe came to our classes so that he could monitor our progress and spent all night sitting on the sidelines laughing like crazy at Brie's antics. We loved having him there, because we could wander over and see him whenever we felt overwhelmed, which was most of the time, and he didn't mind if Brie jumped up or I gazed into his eyes. In fact, he'd often say, "Harry, do you know, you could play Rudolph Valentino." If you don't know who Rudolph Valentino was, he was

this famous "bygone days" (!??!) actor, probably from around the same time as the original RCA dawg, who loved gazing into people's eyes, especially "the ladies," just like I do.

Brie tried to concentrate for as long as she could, but there was something inside her that she didn't seem able to control, and every so often, she'd skitter off to one side of the room and release her pent-up energy as though she had an invisible trampoline beneath her. When she was done, she'd always come back and try as hard as she could to learn our lessons.

At the end of the course, the teacher said Brie should repeat, but she never did, because it was definite now—we were moving to a place called Vietnam, which could be at the end of the earth for all we knew. The night of our graduation (NOT), the teacher did mention to my Mom and Dad that she'd never seen a dog jump as high as Brie, but that was as far as she went with her praise.

The thing that disturbed me was that the teacher never saw Brie do what she did best. It's hard to show your best sometimes, especially when you're feeling under the gun. And I didn't think it was fair, because if the teacher had come with us for our afternoon runs, she would have seen Brie truly soar. Most days we'd go to the emerald-green park near our house so that my Dad could use the Chuckit to throw the ball to the Outer Limits for us.

Now, it's important for you to know that I'd been my Mom's one and only running partner until Brie came into the picture, so running was second nature to me. Every day since I could remember, she'd call out, "Come on, Hars, time to clean out the cobwebs," and off we'd go. When she was getting ready to do a really long run, I'd run with her to keep her company and my Dad would meet us halfway and take me home.

She would even tell my Dad and her friends, in that dreamy voice

she uses when she's going on about us, "it's as though Harry came into the world running," which made me feel very proud. As for tennis balls, they've been one of the most powerful influences in my life so far and fetching them is a skill I've been honing since I was a puppy, so you'll understand that what I'm about to tell you was very hard for me to come to grips with. It meant swallowing my pride, which is not an easy thing to do, and accepting the fact that Brie was a natural athlete beyond anything I could ever aspire to.

This reality check was followed by shock, then gradual acceptance and a kind of bewilderment that came from knowing I *should* feel jealous but didn't. I mean, why wasn't I bothered by this sudden realization that my little sister outshone me by light-years with her natural athleticism and it was Brie, not me, who "came into this world running?" The amazing thing is the answer was there, right in front of me, all the time.

You only had to watch her fly across that field of green once to see that running was the most joyful thing in the world for her, far beyond anything she'd ever dreamed of. I had never seen such complete and utter happiness as I saw in Brie when she ran, and I didn't want anyone or anything to ever take it away from her.

Maybe it was that she'd come out of confinement into a place where she knew she could fly and would always be safe. Maybe she *was* truly born to run. Whatever the reason, it gave her a newfound freedom, and when she was in full flight, she was like a young colt running with the wind. Her coat had changed from the dry, tangled yellow mat it had been when she first came home to a glistening gold, and her tail feathers had filled in and fanned out behind her. She was lean and long-legged, and when she'd run at top speed and leap up to catch the ball mid-air, against all that green, it was truly a magnificent sight to see. She was a Golden in all her splendor, with a spirit as free as a bird soaring toward the heavens and gliding effortlessly back to earth. And there wasn't an ounce of arrogance in her—only pure joy. When my Mom and Dad started calling her Breezie, I thought they couldn't have chosen a more perfect name for her.

I didn't graduate either, and when the teacher talked to my Mom and Dad after the last class, she told them in a very stern tone that I needed "to concentrate more on the task at hand."

"Don't worry, Hars," my Mom said. "You and Breezie were both star finishers!" We sure love our Humans!

CHAPTER 6
Good Morning, Vietnam

The impending move was becoming more visible, with little changes here and there, like my kennel suddenly appearing in the kitchen. And you-know-who was obviously coming too, because her brand-new pink kennel was sitting right next to mine. I was having a very hard time thinking about how she was going to cope being cooped up in the underside of a 747 for hours on end, with no place to get rid of all her energy. In fact, the only way I could deal with it was to put it right out of my mind, which is usually the best approach when you can't get your head around a particularly disturbing thought.

One thing I should point out is that pretty much everything was new for Brie at this stage of her life, so the sudden appearance of our kennels in the kitchen meant ZIP to her, whereas for me, they were a huge red flag signaling "moving van any day now." And sure enough, suddenly, there it was, sitting boldly in the middle of our driveway. After the last of the boxes had been crammed in and the metal bar secured, everyone on our street gathered on our front lawn and stood with somber expressions on their faces, watching the truck pull away. A few people shook hands with my Mom and Dad and mumbled "Good-bye" or "Good luck" under their breath, but most of them were speechless and just loped back to their houses, closing their doors behind them. My Mom said they probably thought we were "nutcases because we were moving to another planet."

My Dad left right away, but Brie and my Mom and I had to wait in an apartment for a few weeks so that we could finish selling Lemon Loaf and give the truck the time it needed to cross the pond. Until you actually get moving, you feel a little bit lost, because you're neither "here" anymore nor "there" yet. Our Humans call this limbo. It's hard to explain except to say it's not a good place to be, so you don't want to stay there for very long. It's like going from nowhere to nowhere, even though you know you're supposed to be going somewhere.

Lemon Loaf finally sold, which meant it was time for us to leave, too, and when the Cathay Pactific man at the airport gave our Mom a nod, she put half a pink pill in my mouth and a whole one in Brie's. After she'd settled Brie into her kennel, she did the same with me, double-checking the latch to make sure it was securely fastened. Just before she left, she crouched down beside me, put her finger through the mesh of my kennel so that she could touch my nose and whispered in my ear, "Look after her, Har," then stood up and walked away. A few minutes later, we were rolling.

I could see Brie in her kennel looking pretty dozy as we moved across the tarmac, and I think she was probably long gone before we were even on the plane. I have only the haziest recollection of our departure myself, which isn't a particularly bad thing. In fact, when I woke up we were already on our way down.

My first whiff as we rolled down the ramp was familiar, but it took one more good long sniff before I could cross-check it in my database and lock it in. Confirmed! We were back in Hong Kong, my old stomping ground. Memories of ARCEA and Tai Tam, Mr. Leung and the rock pools flashed through my brain but vanished the moment we were lifted onto a minivan to begin the most terrifying overland journey in my travels so far. Try as I might, I can think of nothing that comes close to the ride we took that morning with a raving lunatic across the full expanse of Hong Kong's new airport.

There were two things our whacko Chinese minivan driver had to do to get us to our connecting flight to Vietnam. First, he had to swerve dangerously close to every parked airplane in sight to check if it was ours, and second, he had to break every speed record ever set for minivans to ensure he got us there on time. We had no choice but to accept these as part of his job description at the expense of our runaway nerves.

But other things were far beyond accepting OR understanding—for example, why did he insist on waving one hand frantically in the air for the entire trip? Was he signaling for someone to get out of the way? Not likely, because he was the one who was in the way! Screaming into his cell phone and scratchy two-way radio made no sense either, seeing as nothing could be heard above the earth-shattering roar of jet engines.

Besides all the jumbos sitting idly or going to and from the ginormous runways, there were buses, jeeps, carts, fuel and tow trucks, tractors, lifting machines and emergency vehicles with flashing red lights coming at us from every conceivable direction. Finally, after screeching to a halt, backing up and skidding on two wheels around a minivan like ours, we came to a grinding halt. He'd found our plane. Some men helped him with our kennels, and he took off at about a million miles an hour in search of some other poor expat canines to frighten out of their wits.

It felt as though we waited there forever—me with my paws crossed, praying to the Dawg Gawd that our Mom would be on the same plane, and Brie with her anxious little eyes peeking out through the mesh of her kennel, looking as small and frightened as I'd ever seen her. I tried to bring back some memories of my Hong Kong days as a distraction but was much too worried about Brie to think of anything else. The last thing my Mom had asked me to do was look after her, and when your Humans are counting on you, the worst thing in the whole world would be to disappoint them.

I prayed over and over to the Dawg Gawd during the flight, asking him to watch over Brie and when we came to a stop and the power was shut off, I knew my prayers had been answered—whispers of movement behind me. I listened again. A muffled whimper, a few short, shaky breaths, then a long, deep sigh. Relief ran through my body like a cool drink of water on a hot day. After a grueling twenty-four hours huddled all by herself in her kennel, with no idea of when the dawn would come, she was all right. Good morning, Brie, and good morning, Vietnam!

* * *

When the doors opened, it was to a brilliant blue sky and a low scorching sun blazing down, which must have been why the two pretty ladies kneeling beside us on the tarmac were wearing straw hats that looked like the cones the vet makes us wear sometimes. They had long, shiny black hair and beautiful smiles, and I gazed into their eyes for as long as I could hold their attention.

Brie's somber little face flashed by as we were loaded onto a mini-van and driven away from the noise of the planes and the pretty ladies in their hats. As soon as we stopped, our kennels were lifted off the van, carried through a door and plunked down. The men who brought us in disappeared quickly, locking the door behind them, and we were left there, helpless and alone. The air was hot and heavy with a dank, musty smell, making breathing difficult. Flies buzzed all around us, and I had to will myself to put the silent, unseen bugs I knew were crawling beneath us out of my mind. A small crack in the wall allowed a tiny thread of light to slip through and fall on a patch of the dirt floor; otherwise, we were in total darkness. My breathing became short and more labored with the foul odor and stifling heat, and I could hear Brie panting heavily beside me, but there was nothing I could do except lie there and wait.

The occasional roar of a plane found its way inside, but in between, there was silence—no sound of motors or cars, no radios or phones, no voices or sign of Humans, like the gift "scent" from heaven I'd caught when my Mom and Dad came to pick me up in Hong Kong.

Questions and random thoughts began racing through my mind. Where were they? Maybe our Mom wasn't even on our plane, and our Dad wasn't here either. Water? Food? Brie? Who would look after us in this strange, faraway land? Fortunately, common sense kicked in before I allowed these thoughts to unravel me completely.

"Come on, Harry," I said to myself. "You *know* our Mom and Dad are here; in fact, they're somewhere close this very second, trying to figure out what to do. We've just landed in alien territory, for heaven's sake, and there are bound to be a few glitches. They've never let us down—not once in our entire lives—and they're not about to."

I'd just barked an *om mani padme hum*, the mantra I've pretty much memorized from my Mom's yoga CDs, to calm Brie and let her know everything was all right when I heard them. They were speaking in soft, soothing voices through a little cutout in the door, reassuring us that they were there and it wouldn't "be long now." We were on our feet in a flash, wagging, jumping, wiggling and barking uncontrollably. Our ordeal was finally over! We were going home in Vietnam.

Whoops! My radar was scrambling, which generally means something's wrong. It wasn't a dream, and I wasn't imagining it. I was sure of that. They were there. We couldn't see them, but they could see us through the little opening in the door. And we could hear the joy and excitement in their voices telling us how happy they were to be there—apologizing like they always do. They'd run into "a little glitch," but they were "making headway" (?!!?).

Now, do you remember me mentioning the Human tendency to gloss over the truth when they feel it's necessary, making it impossible to get an accurate picture of what's really going on? Well, this tendency was definitely coming into play. If they were actually "making headway," they'd be running through the door that very second, and the fact that they weren't meant the "little glitch" wasn't so little after all.

Silence. Then my Dad's voice, with a kind of musical patter mixed in with it like a singing language with loud, off-key notes and strange clicking noises skipping off tongues.

I had to listen very closely to separate the words he was repeating from the sounds I was hearing in between. Luckily, as the banter went on and my Dad became more and more agitated, his voice rang out loud and clear against the shrill background, and because there were only four words in his tirade, it wasn't hard to pick them up: "inspection," "papers," "key" and "unbelievable"—all that was needed to figure out the "glitch."

"Inspection" and "papers" were the same as Hong Kong, which meant a lady in a white coat with a needle and a man with a stamp must be lurking nearby. I listened again. My Dad's voice had risen to a much higher level, but the words were almost the same as the first time, with the exception of two new ones that I just happened to know: "gone" and "lunch."

WHOA! Had they ever skirted the truth on this one—"little glitch," my paw! The lady and man weren't there at all and everyone else had gone to lunch and wouldn't be back for "two hours," which sounded like another never-ending wait for us. Now I understood where my Dad's "unbelievable!" was coming from. They'd taken the key and there was no one to unlock the door and let us out! He was right. It was unbelievable!

Meanwhile, our Mom was repeating our names, telling us over and over, "Not to worry," that "everything is going to be just fine." But when the brouhaha with my Dad ended abruptly, there was silence, and we didn't hear another word from her.

"VeLLy interesting," I thought to myself. They've gone, vamoosed, skedaddled, and we're on our own again, except this time I could cope with it because I knew they'd be back and I knew we were going to be okay. I gave Brie an "almost good to go" woof.

Sure enough, when they came back, they had a Human solution with them—a key man who immediately started trying out different keys to open the lock. The same musical notes and that clicking sound again: "*Không, Không, Không… Vâng!*" "No, No, No… Yes!"

"*Vâng!*" The door sprang open, and running toward us with outstretched arms and smiling faces were our Mom and Dad, with the key man in hot pursuit. When they were just about to open the doors of our kennels, he jumped forward and blocked them, shouting at the top of his lungs, "*DỪNG! Inspection!*" "STOP, Inspection!"—word number three of your Vietnamese vocabulary, which you can basically ignore unless it comes from your Humans.

They obeyed, stopping dead in their tracks, more out of surprise than anything else, at which point some men appeared out of nowhere and carried us outside, where we saw neither the lady with the needle nor the man with the stamp, just a small stone-faced gathering of Vietnamese officials (?!!?), our Mom and Dad, and Brie and me, still in our kennels, ten hundred hours plus a day after our departure from Canada.

Gradually, more and more Humans appeared and stood gawking, their eyes fixed on us and expressions of curiosity and/or holy terror on their faces. A few brave souls shuffled forward slowly and squatted down to get a closer look before backing away, their mouths gaped open in amazement. Moments later, the number had grown to a much larger group of motley Humans, none of them with papers, needles or stamps for inspection. The new ones approached in much the same way as the others, inching forward, peering hesitantly into our kennels, then backing up quickly. Everyone seemed incapable of speaking, even the key man, who finally walked over to my Dad and waved his hand dismissively in the air, signaling "Inspection finish. Go!"

Thus concluded our clearance into Vietnam.

Whoops! I forgot one thing. They'd taken my Mom's passport and no one had any idea where it was.

* * *

I know I can't adequately put into words how we felt when we were finally reunited with our Mom and Dad after our long, hard journey, but I'm going to try, because I want you to get an idea of how far beyond "normal happiness" it's possible to go.

If you were to take every Golden, heartwarming life experience you've ever had and extract the feeling each one brought you, then put them all together so that they melded into one, you'd get a sense of that moment. For me, it was the feeling of wonder when I first encountered snow, the thrill of swimming in the surf and flying along the catchments with ARCEA in Hong Kong, the excitement that charges through my body before a run and the happiness of seeing my Mom and Dad walk through our gate every single day.

For Brie, I'm sure it was the same: the relief she felt when she came home from the shelter to a place where she knew she'd be safe; the feeling she has when she's in full flight, running across a field of green and leaping into the air for the absolute love of it; and the palpable joy she gets from everything around her.

The second they opened the doors to our kennels, we were out, our faces beaming, our backsides wiggling and squirming with glee, our tails wagging with unconditional love as we rubbed against our Mom and Dad, pushing our noses between their legs so they could scratch our ears and ruffle the fur around our necks, scrunching up our shoulders, burying our heads deeper and deeper into them, nuzzling closer and closer, and feeling the warmth and gentleness in their hands as they kneaded and stroked and massaged our backs. You couldn't possibly have found two happier, more contented dawgs or Humans in the whole world at that moment.

When we finally untangled ourselves, we knew there were some things that required our immediate attention. First, we had to pee and HOW, which took no time at all because of a complete absence of water during our long ordeal. By far the most urgent need was to replenish what we'd missed and what our bodies were crying out for, so when a jolly-looking man named Mr. Gary Dale appeared with two enormous bowls filled to the brim, it was like rain after an endless drought. Nothing in my life had ever tasted as good as that clear, ice-cold water, and we drank like we'd never drunk before, curling our tongues up and scooping it into our mouths, taking long, sloppy gulps, splashing it everywhere, not even pausing to have our bowls refilled; instead, throwing our heads back and letting the water flow into our mouths freely as it was being poured, then lapping it up as fast as we could.

When we couldn't possibly drink one more drop, we lifted our heads and took a good long look at Mr. Gary Dale for the very first time, locking our eyes directly into his with our deepest gratitude. His grin was almost as wide as Brie's, and his twinkling eyes were smiling down at us with inexplicable warmth and affection. "Well, well, well," he said in a voice as kind as his face. "Aren't you somethin'! A pleasure to meet you, Mister Harry and Miss Brie, and welcome to Hanoi!" We were over the moon!

He led us all to a waiting van, and as soon as we were settled—Brie and me in the very back and our Mom and Dad and Mr. Gary Dale in the seats behind the driver—we pulled out and headed away from the airport.

One of the first things that hit me was the loud, non-stop honking coming from every vehicle on the road, including ours; in fact, I'm almost certain the driver kept his hand on the horn from the time we left the airport until we arrived at our new house. It didn't seem to matter whether he was just thinking about passing another car, taxi, truck, motorbike, pushbike, Human, pig, duck, cow, goat or chicken; was actually doing it; or was just cruising down the open road with nothing in front of him—in other words, nothing to even consider passing. But he kept right on honking all the same.

Fact No. 1, from my Dad: "There are 33 million (?!!?) legally registered vehicles on the road in Vietnam. Of these, 1.3 million are cars and 31 million are motorbikes. This doesn't include the zillions that no one's supposed to know about."

Fact No. 2, from yours truly, Harry Howard: At any given time, *most* of these vehicles are on the same road, honking at the same time. And a huge number of them just happen to be on the same road that we are.

Fact No. 3, from yours truly again: It drives all Human expats living in Vietnam totally bonkers!

After we'd crossed a big bridge, there were beautiful open stretches of green, shimmering like watery silk, with pretty ladies in their straw hats bent over in the fields working in the scorching heat of the afternoon sun. Once we turned off the main road, there were hardly any cars, and we had to crawl along at a snail's pace, because the road was bumpy and the driver had to maneuver his way through swarms of motorbikes and scooters, all honking like crazy and jostling for position, with entire families on the back of one bike: a small boy against his Dad's chest in front, his arms stretched out as far as they could go, barely reaching the handlebars; two little girls tucked in behind, one with her arms around her Dad's waist, the other around her sisters; and at the very back, their Mom holding a tiny baby in her lap.

A lot of motorbikes didn't have any Humans on them except for the driver, just chickens and ducks hanging loosely over the sides, strung together with bits of rope, or pigs crowded together in wooden carts being pulled from behind.

There were children everywhere, laughing and playing near the side of the road or darting out lithely into the endless stream of traffic to scramble for a ball that had gotten away or jump on the back of a friend's bicycle; old men huddled together around little plastic tables, women selling drinks in bottles and young boys selling gasoline in bottles that looked like drinks. Pretty girls with baskets of flowers rode beside us or stood near stalls with colorful stacks of fruit; and piles of shiny green watermelons were seen around every curve, teetering as though they were about to fall.

Without a whole lot of thought, my Dad suddenly decided to open the windows to give us some fresh air. I think he just got carried away with the moment, which can happen, but given everything out there, not to mention Brie's habit of leaning out of the car window as far as she can and my inclination to stand up on the back seat and bark manically whenever she does, it was a pretty weird thing to do.

Brie and I had been staring at some chickens and roosters all jammed together in a cage on the other side of the road, so we didn't see the enormous Brahma bulls beside the van until the driver was *almost* past them but not quite almost enough, if you get my drift. Too late—we'd spotted them. As if we wouldn't have. I mean, there was an entire herd right beside us!

You can imagine. Sorry, sorry, I take that back. You can't begin to! Total pandemonium broke out in the van, with me standing up on the seat barking louder than I thought was possible, and my Dad and Mr. Gary Dale trying to haul Brie back inside and hold her down. Luckily, the driver managed to find an opening quite quickly, but the bulls were pressed up against the side of the van like a formidable force until we got past them and the van could easily have toppled over. I don't think my crazed barking was just because of Brie, either. I mean, everything was so far beyond anything we'd ever seen. My Mom, who had turned a ghostly white and appeared to be in total shock, suddenly blurted out, "My Gawd, we've been living in a bubble for our entire lives!" If they had, what about Brie and me, whose only "live" encounters so far had been with the ducks in the duck pond at the Dawg Park, a few seagulls, the dawg friends we'd made and the odd cat besides Chibi, who was more like a dawg anyway.

We've since learned that size commands a great deal of respect and that the rules for expat canines on first sighting a Brahma bull, cow or water buffalo must be followed to a tee— no ifs, ands or buts— whether you're in a car or simply attempting to pass one or a group on a morning run.

Rule No. 1: No barking, jumping or lunging under any circumstances.

Rule No. 2: If you're in a car, hit the floor and stay low.

Rule No. 3: On foot, acknowledge your Human's command by cutting back to a calm, ree-laxed saunter.

Rule No. 4: Bow your head reverently as you pass, avoiding eye contact.

Rule No. 5: Wait for your Human's next command and OBEY!

These same rules can also be used with elephants, though they can go sideways pretty easily because of shock over their humungous size. We experienced this in Chiangmai, when we were at the gas station with our Dad and two huge elephants lumbered past, then stopped by the side of the road. For some strange reason, which once again completely escapes me, our Dad thought it would be a good idea for Brie and me to "experience elephants"(?!!?)—at least I think that's what he told our Mom. HULLO! Did he not learn *anything* from the Hanoi incident?

As soon as we were out of the car, Rule No. 1 went straight out the window on all three counts, with wild, defiant barking; leaping instead of jumping; and diving as opposed to lunging. We even dragged our Dad along with us until we were right up against the elephants' colossal backsides and went totally berserk when a trunk swooped down, grabbed some bananas and shoved them into an enormous mouth. I don't know how he did it, but our Dad managed to pull us away and drag us back to the car. His teeth were clenched all the way home, and he was dripping with sweat.

There was no anger or raised voices after the encounter with the Brahma bulls. Mr. Gary Dale simply whipped some snacks out of his pocket and offered them to us in the same gentle manner he'd greeted us with at the airport, then told my Dad those "damn cows" were always on the road. He had a very gentle, calming way about him; I mean, he could have even been a dog whisperer for all we knew. My Dad says "he's a true Southern gentleman," which sounds like the best kind of Human you can be.

The rest of the trip was incident free, with Brie and me lying on the back seat, enjoying our treats, and our Mom and Dad and Mr. Gary Dale talking quietly in front of us. The next thing we knew, we were pulling up in front of our house on West Lake. A thin rain was falling, and it was almost dark.

CHAPTER 7
Hanoi

We had to stick pretty close to home after we arrived in Hanoi, because of jet lag and our Mom and Dad's culture shock, so our outings were fairly short and not to the lake or the field on the other side of our road. It was summertime, and when the rains came, the water was dark and choppy, especially if there was a typhoon nearby. In the beginning, the lake was even out of bounds on clear days, and the closest we could get to it was by flopping down on the big window seats in the front room and looking mournfully out over the water.

We didn't have a real garden like we do in Ho Chi Minh City, but we had a roof garden on the very top of our house, where we could go if our Mom and Dad were with us. Otherwise, it was a "no go," and the door was kept locked. The coolest thing was a covered play area we discovered on our first tear through the garden the night we arrived in Mr. Gary Dale's van. It went from the front to the back, and the most awesome thing about it wasn't the area itself but what was in it. WHOA! Did we luck out on this one!

The people who lived in the house before us had eight black-and-yellow birds that they'd left in cages hanging from the ceiling, and Brie and I could sit there and bark at them all day long if we

wanted to, while they squawked back. It was like being in a real live band, and because our barks are distinctively different in tone and the birds' screeches were different in pitch, we caused quite a ruckus in the neighborhood! They were the perfect distraction to get us through Stage Two of culture shock, when our Mom's too afraid to go past the end of the street and doesn't know how to talk to anyone. Actually, I think the birds might have helped her turn the corner and get us back to our regular running routine. She couldn't stand the racket any longer.

Hanoi was a new beginning for all of us. It was Brie's first posting as an expat canine, and she approached it in the same way she does everything—with pure joy and wonder. It was here that she not only discovered geckos for the very first time but where she started her nightly patrols, going a little farther each day until she was scouring the entire house, even the upper reaches of the walls.

Once we started going out, our adventures became more frequent and bizarre than we'd ever experienced before. I think it's the same for Human expats in Vietnam; it seems to just come with the territory. The yappy little street dogs bothered us at first, but after we started ignoring them, they left us alone. The Poodle with the attitude moved back to wherever she came from, which left only one vicious German Shepherd that we had to pass on our way to Quang Ba, the lake we swam in most days. He scared us so much that we ended up changing our route and taking twice as long to get there. When our Dad heard about it, he decided he was going to put a stop to it "once and for all," and as the dawg came running toward us one morning, growling and baring his teeth, he started jumping up and down, waving our orange Chuckit in the air and making these wild cries like a complete madman. "Take that and that and that," he shouted at the dawg, who took one look at him and flew back into his garden. Afterward, I heard him say to my Mom in one of those deep, gruff voices you hear on TV, "Hmmph— try that, and he'll never bother you again!" But we stuck to the longer way. We didn't need to be frightened to within an inch of our lives every single day.

Other run-ins weren't with dawgs; they were with shady-looking men, lurking in the shadows on the way to Quang Ba. Our Mom and Dad had been warned to watch out for these evil-minded Humans[6] but were visibly shaken when they saw them.

The first encounter was just before the turnoff to the lake one morning when we were running with our Mom. A man suddenly appeared out of nowhere, waving a bunch of money in front of her. There was something about his expressionless face and his cold gray eyes that made my radar click in as soon as I saw him. He spoke quickly in that strange language we'd been hearing, and even though our Mom couldn't understand a word he was saying, she knew exactly what he wanted. She immediately tightened her grip on our leads and, when she'd put some distance between him, turned and shouted something back over her shoulder. One word rang out above the rest—"PO-LEECE"—and as soon as he heard it, he shifted his feet nervously and put the money back in his pocket. In the next breath, we were racing home.

The minute we walked in the door, she phoned our Dad. We didn't have to go on a wild taxi ride to the vet, but it was still an emergency, and from then on, we could never let down our guard. Different men would appear at the same spot, and our nerves would stand on end as soon as we saw them. They were part of something the Human expats in Hanoi called the "Dawg Mafia" (?!!?), and everyone cringed when the words were spoken. Sometimes, they'd drive by in a truck or even on a motorbike, grab dawgs off the road and speed away. Other

---

6 Locals who offer money and/or snatch dogs that are then sold, butchered and eaten. The insatiable appetite for dog meat in Vietnam, fuels this cruel practice, which is still common, especially in the north. It is estimated that more than a million dogs are consumed every year in Vietnam, many during Tet, Vietnamese New Year, when "consumption peaks to around 252,000 in Hanoi alone."

times, they'd wave money in the air like they did with us. If there had been another route, we would have taken it.

There was a different kind of incident with the Dawg Mafia that happened not long after we arrived in Hanoi that put all the Human expats in West Lake on high alert. We were chilling out after dinner one night, when we heard our Mom and Dad talking in their hushed, no-nonsense voices about something that had happened "recently."

According to my Dad, there had been a "dawg-napping in West Lake." The Dawg Mafia "had broken into a very important Japanese man's house, taken his dawg, and were holding it for ransom" (?!!?), which made it "a hostage situation." After they took the dawg, they sent the man a letter asking for a lot of dong to get it back. I don't know if the dong was for the PO-LEECE or the Dawg Mafia, but my Dad says, "It doesn't matter, because everyone pays and everyone's on the take," whatever that means. The best part was that the dawg was returned safely. The men who had taken him disappeared mysteriously and were never seen again. My Dad called it "rough justice" (?!!?). Go figure.

Needless to say, we weren't ever allowed out by ourselves, not even to futz around in front of our house. Thankfully, we had the birds, the oversized mice we'd seen scampering near their cages recently (AKA rats) and each other.

* * *

Everyone else we met in West Lake was smiling and friendly: the children who called out "*xin chào, dẹp* and *tam biệt*" (hello, beautiful and good-bye) whenever they saw us; the young girls in their conical hats, selling fruit and flowers from baskets on the backs of their bicycles; the broom man with his zany, happy-go-lucky music and his cart filled with stick brooms and soft, feathered ones he'd tickle our noses with; and the young boys carrying back-breaking loads of earth to plant the orange trees for Tet. They'd work in the fields all day long and still be there at night, using tiny white lights so they could see. If we went for a walk after dinner, they'd all smile and call out *xin chào,* as if they weren't even tired. At New Year's, zillions of people would come to buy their trees, and you'd see them strapped on the back of motorbikes zooming all over Hanoi.

One of the most amazing revelations for us was the roadside cuisine,[7] just waiting for us to come along and help ourselves. It was as though we'd crossed the pond to this idyllic land where all the food we love was up for grabs: mango pits, slices of watermelon, chicken bones, half-eaten cobs of corn, baguettes, rice—the wonder of it was almost too much to grasp.

In the early mornings, we'd wake to the delicious smells of freshly baked bread drifting by outside and hear the familiar sound of the *bánh mì* lady's bell as she came by the house on her bicycle selling her warm baguettes. Our Mom would usually buy an extra one and divvy it up so that Brie and I would each get half, but sometimes I couldn't wait, so I'd take one out of her basket to make things easier for everyone. This immediately prompted a piercing, "Why, Hareeeeee? Why????" from my Mom, followed by a tongue-lashing that I "knew better." I mean, what exactly was supposed to register here? She'd pay the *bánh mì* lady extra for my baguette, so it wasn't like I was stealing from her. Honest to Dawg—it's a real challenge to figure out where your Humans are coming from at times.

After we discovered the lake at Quang Ba, we went almost every day, running past the flower farms and up the hill to the farmer's shack. As soon as we got there, our Mom would let us off our leads and we'd tear down the other side to the lake.

Brie's athleticism in the water seemed to enter a whole new phase when she got to Hanoi. She took on this air of showmanship, bursting

---

7 Food left out on the side of the road for stray dogs, a common practice throughout Asia.

with energy and joyful playfulness as she leapt into the air—forward, backwards, sideways, straight up, every single leap different from the one before. Later, she added this kind of spinner twist after she shot out of the water, turning her head and looking back over her shoulder to see if anyone was watching. She even taught herself to duck dive, disappearing beneath the surface then springing up out of the lake with her legs splayed like a gecko.

Her finale would come when it was time to leave. My Mom would call her, but she'd pretend she didn't hear and keep doing whatever she was doing—jumping, twisting and turning, cutting through the water with the speed and confidence of a true performer. We'd run up the path and hide behind the bushes where she couldn't see us, and eventually, it would dawn on her that we might have actually gone. Two shakes and she'd come charging up the bank to where we were waiting, grinning from ear to ear.

On the way home, we'd cross the road that led to a farmer's market. Brie would lunge at the baskets covering the chickens, and everyone would laugh, except the chickens. If we kept going, we'd reach the open fields that swept down to the tall grasses on the banks of the Red River. The river was much too wide and too fast for us to swim in, so we'd stop and rest on a soft spot on the top of the hill where we could look down at the boat ladies in their conical hats, poling their way downstream. Sometimes, our Mom would start talking to us as if we were Human, like she does, and we'd concentrate as hard as we could so she'd think we really were. Other times, no words were spoken and we'd lie there on the grass, watching the river go by and the water swirling with its gold and silver light, a trio of happiness.

* * *

The restrictions on swimming in West Lake in front of our house and running through the paddy field across the road were finally lifted so we could swim close to home and take a shortcut to Quang Ba, but this newfound freedom was short-lived.

The first mishap was mine when we were cutting across the field. Our Mom would stay on the raised ridges of earth that ran around the outside of the paddies and down the middle while Brie and I ran below, where we could jump and splash in the puddles. If I was thirsty, I'd stop and drink from a rut on the edge of the paddy, then run up along the ridge to the road where Brie and my Mom would be waiting.

On the day of my accident, they were fidgety when I got there. Okay, so I'd been a little longer than usual at the drink station, but I was there now and we could go, except suddenly my legs gave out from underneath me, and I was on the ground. I managed to get up, but then the pain came, gripping my stomach so tightly I couldn't stand it, and I went down again, shuddering and shaking and spilling out everything inside. My Mom was there in a heartbeat, holding my head and rubbing my tummy to try to ease the pain, but it wouldn't stop, and I lay there, unable to move, getting sicker and sicker. I could see the worry on my Mom's face, but when she spoke her voice was firm. "I know how much it hurts, Har," she said, "but you're going to have to help me get you home. I can't do it by myself." And so, ever so slowly, we made our way along the upper ridge of the field, with Brie tagging behind, and every so often, I'd find myself on the ground again, wishing I could stay there forever, but my Mom wouldn't let me. She'd help me up and coax me on a little bit farther. When we finally reached the gate, she carried me inside, rushed to the phone and called my Dad and a taxi.

We drove to the university, where we met Dr. Die for the very first time. I was afraid at first, but when he held my head in his hands so that I was looking directly into his eyes, I wasn't afraid anymore. His face was gentle, and his eyes were warm silver and full of kindness. His helpers lifted me up onto the cold table and he put a needle in my leg and tied it to a bottle. Then he spoke quietly to my Mom. She told me he was going to do something that would hurt and make me "as sick as a dawg" (?!!?), but afterward, she'd be right there with me, and I'd feel better. Then she held me down while he put a tube into my tummy. I yelped as it went in, but almost immediately after I was all right. He ruffled the fur behind my ears, gave my Mom a reassuring nod and left the room.

I kept on being as sick as a dawg, like I was supposed to be for a long time. Sometime later, my Dad appeared and kept vigil with my Mom while Brie slept soundly nearby. My memory of everything afterward is cloudy. I think I stayed at Dr. Die's hospital for more than a few days and nights and slept through most of them. Sometimes, it felt as if Brie and my Mom came in and out of my dreams, but they weren't dreams. They were with me every day until the sun faded in the sky and my Dad came. And they were there again in the morning.

Dr. Die found some bugs inside me that dawgs and Humans get from dirty water. There was also something the farmer had put on his field, so we never took that shortcut again. When I came home, the only thing I was allowed to eat was *cháo* (rice porridge), which was a far cry from our mouth-watering sticky rice, but you have to eat what your Mom gives you when you've been sick. The highlight was going in a taxi every day so that Dr. Die could check to make sure the bugs were gone. After a few trips, he told my Mom and Dad that "HaLLy okay and veLLy **R**ucky," but I think Brie was the **R**ucky one, because she didn't drink the water—even though she had her own misfortune shortly after mine.

The days were still warm, but the nights were misty and it was getting colder in Hanoi. We were at the beach in front of our house and Brie was practicing a new routine where she'd bounce in and out of the water a little ways offshore, leap into the air, touch down and push off from the bottom to get maximum height. As usual, she was the perfect little performer and couldn't have cared less about anything around her, but as we were standing watching her get ready to launch herself for the umpteenth time, she suddenly let out a piercing cry. When my Dad ran in and carried her out of the water, her paw was bright red and she was whimpering and yelping in pain.

My Mom tore up a towel and wrapped it around her foot, while my Dad called a taxi to go to Dr. Die. His helpers lifted her onto the table, just like they'd done with me, and held her while he put a needle into her paw. When she cried out, my Dad put his fist into her mouth for her to bite down on. One paw was embedded with big pieces of glass from the bottom of the lake, and after he'd taken it all out, Dr. Die wrapped her foot with a bandage, spoke softly to my Mom and Dad, and gave them some medicine for Brie. She slept with her head on my Mom's lap all the way home and didn't do much of anything that day, except lie on the window seat and stare out at the boats between long, deep sleeps.

We were all amazed to see her come hopping into the kitchen on three legs the next morning as if she'd been doing it all her life, and right after breakfast, she was moving all over the house—up and down the stairs to badger the birds, even scrambling up on the sofas and beds. A taxi ride a few days later to get her bandages off and she was as good as new.

* * *

Just before Brie's accident, we'd discovered a place out along West Lake where all sorts of Vietnamese Humans went to fish. It was a pretty little bay with small bamboo huts in the water and little bridges to get to them. People would sit with their feet hanging over the edge of their decks, holding their lines and waiting for a fish to bite, though they didn't seem to really care if they caught one or not. I think it was the peace and quiet they loved more than anything, far from the blaring horns of motorbikes, cars and buses, and the madding crowd. Some of them didn't even bother with fishing lines; they just came to ree-lax or play pool at the tables outside, and if they wanted food, they could eat at the restaurant.

For us, it was pretty much tied for first for "Best Outing of the Week" along with swimming at Quang Ba. We'd fly around the shoreline where the lake was calm, checking out who was there, bounding in and out of the water and rolling in the grass afterward with happiness that was impossible to contain.

The very first time we went, we met a beautiful young girl named Phuong, who became one of our VBFs in Hanoi, but it was different with Phuong than it was with our other VBFs, the difference being, we were head over heels in love with her, and I mean gaga. The only thing we could do when we saw her was stand and stare with goofy grins on our faces and the sun, the moon and the stars shining in our eyes. The minute she saw us, her face would light up and she'd call out, "*Xin chào*, HaLLy. *Xin chào,* BLie," rolling our names off her tongue like smooth silk. If she wasn't too busy, we'd sit at her feet near the lake while she massaged our backs and ruffled the fur on our necks, whispering "*dep dep*" into our ears and talking to our Mom. And all the time, we'd keep moving closer and closer so that we could gaze directly into her eyes, and she'd see how smitten we were.

When we went back to see her after Brie's leg was better, we were surprised to find a green cage in the middle of the courtyard beside the restaurant with two black furry animals inside. Their coats were short but thick, and they were slouched over in opposite corners of the cage, looking very lonely and uncomfortably hot. They had yellow sun-shaped bibs on their chests and the same-colored mark on their muzzles, and even though they were a lot fatter than us, they weren't much taller. Their ears were round, like mice ears but of course much bigger, and they had very long, sharp claws. They were bears!

We'd never seen real live bears before, and these weren't just any old bears, they were sun bears, which my Mom says are "very exotic." Phuong told her they're the smallest bears in the world and are sometimes called dawg bears, which almost made them seem like part of our family.

To this day, I have no idea what our Mom could possibly have been thinking when she led us to within a hair of their cage, but I'm guessing it was one of those "getting carried away with the moment" things like my Dad's. Normally, she's very cautious and wouldn't do anything like that, but this was right up there on the same level as him opening the window of Mr Gary Dale's van to "give us some fresh air," when it really had nothing to do with us and everything to do with him wanting a better view of the total chaos on the road. It was no different with my Mom and the sun bears. She clearly had her heart set on seeing them at close range.

When I compare the incident with the Brahma bulls and the van, I have to say it was veLLy veLLy different, the most terrifying difference being that we weren't "in" the van. We were "out there," within spitting distance of a cage with two bears in it and a very good chance of direct contact.

We were also dealing with bears, not bulls, which we knew nothing about. To even think of the two incidents in the same light is absurd; we were a hundred million times closer to the edge on this one. Aside from our completely out-of-control barking and leaping and lunging, we were in a raging war of resistance against our Mom, who was trying desperately to pull us back and put enough space between us and the bears to prevent a real tragedy.

When they stood up on their hind legs, with their long, sharp claws sticking out through the bars almost touching Brie's nose, and started rattling the cage so hard it looked like it was going to fall over, Brie stood down faster than she'd ever done in her life. A few panic-stricken twirls to get our bearings before we screamed out of there, running at a full gallop all the way home. Great drama in the retelling over dinner that night! Our Mom was clearly as unnerved as we were.

Despite the trauma, I thought about those little dawg bears a lot, slumped over in the corners of their cage day after day in the sweltering heat. It could be they were as frightened of us as we were of them. The next time we went back, we were surprised to see that they

were gone. Phuong told my Mom they'd caught colds and had to go to the hospital, but somehow it didn't fit. A little later, I overheard "Dawg Mafia" in one of those hush-hush conversations and pictured the bears all by themselves, scared to death. I had to shrug off the thought that came next. [8]

The rest of our days in Hanoi were bright and carefree, spent running and swimming in our favorite places, enjoying the wonderful variety of roadside cuisine, watching the orange trees speeding away on the backs of motorbikes, taking leisurely walks with our Mom and Dad and all the children we'd befriended, and whiling away the afternoons on our window seats looking out over the lake. We still badgered the birds, though some of them had mysteriously disappeared, so our jam sessions weren't as lively as they'd been with the original big band.

I'm not sure exactly when we left Hanoi, but suddenly there we were, being rolled up a ramp onto another plane bound for parts unknown. I do remember the orange trees had come and gone, because we could run through the empty fields, so it must have been after Tet.

Good morning, good evening and *tam biệt* (good-bye), Vietnam!

---

8 The bears' bile is extracted from the gallbladder and sold for traditional Chinese medicine, or the gallbladder is extracted and sold. It comes at a terrible cost to the bears, who are imprisoned in tiny cages, and the physical and mental suffering they endure is extreme. Sun bear meat is also eaten by indigenous people.

CHAPTER 8
The Land of Smiles

I'll begin by explaining that our time in Thailand was a layover between Hanoi and Ho Chi Minh City that lasted for a few years so that my Mom could get on with her business in Chiangmai and my Dad could get on with his in Vietnam. We missed our Dad like crazy, but he came to visit us often, and the best thing would be going to meet him at the airport and hanging out with the Golden sniffer dawg whose name was Nam. If you're a sniffer dawg in Thailand, you spend most of your time flopped out in front of the airport, waiting for friends like Brie and me to come and play with you. We never saw Nam sniff anything besides us—not once.

Our entry into Chiangmai was about as casual and unofficial as you could get. As soon as our kennels came off the plane, we were carried toward the airport and set down on a kind of raised rubber walkway. It was the strangest thing. There was a slow metallic groan and then the whole thing started moving with Brie and me on it. One minute we were outside, and the next we were going through a breezy flap in the wall into a brightly lit room, round and round with all the bags—inside, outside, inside again—until two men finally came and lifted us off. Our Mom eventually showed up, unlatched our kennels

and clipped on our leashes. No inspection, no nothing. Our empty kennels went on a cart with our other bags, and when we got outside, a man named Tui, was waiting for us. I'm not sure how my Mom knew Tui, but from that night on, he was our VBF in Chiangmai.

We made quite a few new friends in Chiangmai besides Tui and Ohmsin, but they were our absolutely best Thai friends. That's Ohmsin with us on our front porch. She came every day on her motorbike, and in the winter, she wore a black mask over her head, so all you could see were her eyes. It wasn't even cold in Chiangmai, but my Humans say, "It's what you're used to." So if it's been hotter than Hades and the temperature suddenly falls off, everyone bundles up like Ohmsin. We can always tell when Humans love us to bits, and Ohmsin loved us almost as much as our Mom and Dad. And we sure loved Ohmsin.

I don't remember having any culture shock in Thailand, and I'm pretty sure our Mom and Dad didn't either, because I didn't see a single outburst or meltdown. I think the reason is that everything in Thailand has to be *mai bpen rai,* which means "no problem, it doesn't matter, never mind, and don't mention it"—all at the same time. In other words, you can't worry about ANYTHING, and to make absolutely sure no one does, there's this rule that's like a royal decree for the entire country. No matter what happens, you always have to smile, and I mean 24/7. So that's what we did when we lived in Chiangmai. We spent almost every waking moment flashing winning smiles at anyone and everyone we saw.

Besides no culture shock because of *mai bpen rai,* there were a lot of other very cool things about living in Chiangmai. One of the best was our Mom's car and being able to go everywhere she went. I'd co-pilot up front with my head on her shoulder, and Brie would stand up on the back seat with her entire upper body hanging out the window and her ears pressed flat against her head. Usually we'd just go for spins around town, but when my Dad came back from Vietnam, we went for long drives up into the mountains, stopping for swims and fried bananas on the way.

Another best thing about Chiangmai was our house, which was much more in the country than it was in the city. Everywhere we went, smiling Thai Moms and Dads and children would call out *"Sawasdee kha* (hello) HaLLy" and *"Sawasdee kha,* BLee," which is how a lot of people in Thailand and Vietnam say our names. They even call my Mom, JuRie and Sara, SaLa, when she comes to visit.

In the early morning, we'd run out the gate along the *klongs* (canals) past the open fields and orchid farms, until we came to a beautiful, fragrant forest that we'd cut through to get to our favorite swimming place—a small lake surrounded by lush grasses and tall palms, with a little hut on one side, a farmer's house on the other and a glittering Thai temple on the top of the hill.

* * *

Our first incident in Chiangmai was a feathered one and is still a bit of a blur, because it happened so fast I barely had time to catch my breath. Our Mom had let us off our leads so that we could run ahead and go for our Dunlops as soon as she threw them in the lake, and we were almost there when Brie's radar clicked in. In the blink of an eye, she was gone, screaming off in the direction of the farmer's house, ducking under the fence, leaving nothing but a swirling cloud of dust in her path. The only sounds we heard for the next sliver of time were high-pitched screeches and squawks coming from behind a grove of trees, until she flew out in a mad flurry, racing toward the lake as fast as her legs would carry her. To our utter astonishment, clutched in her mouth was the biggest rooster you've ever laid eyes on, its feathers draped across her chest like an enormous boa, its tiny head and legs buried somewhere in its disheveled mass of plumage. Directly behind her came the farmer in hot pursuit, shouting at the top of his lungs and trying for all he was worth to close the gap between them.

When they first came into view, my Mom was so horrified that all she could do was stand with her feet riveted to the ground and her mouth wide open, staring in disbelief. Then, ever so slowly, she drew her hands up over her face and covered her eyes so she wouldn't have to watch for one more second. But she must have felt terrible guilt for the ruckus Brie was causing, along with a sense of duty to see it through and do whatever she could to let the farmer know how sorry she was, because when I looked again, she'd taken her hands away from her eyes and was watching the incredible finale in progress with the same incredulous look on her face. Brie, still clinging to the rooster as if her life depended on it, had suddenly spotted a tennis ball in the lake and was coming in for a spectacular landing not far from us. The fluorescent ball seemed to be flashing in front of her like a beacon on a dark night, commanding her to abort her mission—NOW!

Without missing a beat, she dropped that poor little creature like a hot potato and kept on going, with nothing on her mind but the ball and her instinctive need to rescue it. There was no hesitation, not even a brief pause. She just leapt into the water, without a care in the world, and started swimming to her heart's content, a picture of pure and absolute joy, completely unaware of the rooster, the farmer, my Mom or me.

Meanwhile, the rooster lay motionless by the edge of the lake, with the farmer and my Mom crouched over him. Ever so carefully, the farmer picked him up, cradled him in his arms and walked slowly toward the hut. My Mom followed. No words were spoken, but they were there, somewhere between the sad, remorseful look on my Mom's face and the farmer's gentle hands. I crept a little closer to get a better look and was relieved to see the rooster's wet, matted feathers quivering and his tiny little chest pulsing underneath. In spite of the trauma, he seemed all right, though his morning wake-up call may have been lost forever. My Dad says he'd like "to rip the voice box out of the roosters that live next door to us now," which doesn't sound like a very charitable thing to do.

Shortly after Brie's first feathered encounter, she had another. We'd been invited to our neighbor's house for tea, and Brie had been running back and forth across the lawn, bounding in and out of the flower beds since we got there. Suddenly, she disappeared behind some bushes, emerging in the next breath with a pretty good–sized chicken hanging out of her mouth. I took off with two little boys who had been playing in the garden, and we tore after her, skidding around the corners, spewing dust and dirt everywhere. After a few exhausting laps, she stopped, dropped the chicken, flopped down on the ground, panting and catching her breath, then began rolling in the grass in ecstasy. Throughout the entire episode, the Humans just sat on the verandah with detached expressions on their faces, calmly sipping their tea as if they couldn't have cared less. But someone must have, because we were never invited back. My Mom said, "We burnt our bridges" (!??!), whatever that means. The chicken was shaken but all in one piece.

* * *

Our VBF Tui used to visit us regularly in Chiangmai, and as soon as we'd hear the familiar *putt-putt* of his shiny blue *tuk-tuk* (three-wheeled motorized taxis so named because of the sound of their engines), which was about the coolest thing we'd ever seen, we'd run to the gate to greet him, then jump and prance alongside as he drove in the driveway. Brie, who has this habit of dragging her towel with her whenever she's excited, would immediately start whipping it back and forth to let Tui know how happy she was to see him, while I'd wiggle and wag him over to our morning meeting place. It was always the same with Tui. He'd pull out a bag of fried bananas and after we'd given him a high five and he'd given us two or three, he'd say *"set lao!"* which means "all gone" in Thai. The thing was, Brie and I knew Tui inside out, and he always had an extra bag in his back pocket. We also knew our puppy dawg eyes had the same effect on Tui as they've had on Humans everywhere! A wink, a grin and VOILÀ, the second bag of those tasty little morsels would appear.

When Tui was busy in the garden, his *tuk-tuk* would sit in our driveway and he'd let us stay in it for as long as we wanted, which could be our entire afternoon naptime if nothing else was going on. When he'd finished what he was doing, he'd take us for a spin around our *moo baan* (gated community), which was usually the best thing that happened that day. Tui was always telling me I was *"pum pui,"* which means roly-poly in Thai, but I didn't care, because he was my VBF in all of Thailand.

One day when Tui had come to hang out with us in the garden, he spotted some shredded skin beside the stones and bamboo at the edge of the pond below our front porch. As soon as he saw it, he knew we had an uninvited guest—as in a twelve-foot-long python that was much too close for comfort. He immediately called his friend Bamm.

It was a sweltering day in the middle of rainy season, and the grass was drenched from the summer downpours, so the incident wasn't all that surprising when you think of a perfect habitat. My Mom said, "That snake obviously knew a good thing when he saw it," and "We might as well hang a sign outside our gate saying 'Python B&B—everyone welcome'!"

Brie, my Mom and I watched from the window as Tui and Bamm lifted the rocks away from the tall grass on one side of the pond. When the snake wormed his way out of the water a few minutes later, Bamm raised a huge club over his head and brought it down with all his strength. For the next little while, all we could see were the two men hunched over the ground, their back and arm muscles tight and soaked in sweat as they strained to hold on to the squirming coils. Suddenly, Tui was on his feet, holding an enormous sack that was pitching and rolling with the weight inside. It looked as though that snake had enough fight to come hissing and spitting right back out, but after a few minutes, his movement subsided.

Our Mom inched her way over and stood on her tiptoes, peering into the sack before Bamm tied it with rope and put it in the back of his truck. She was clearly undone, because her face was all scrunched up and her teeth stayed clenched for the rest of the day. When she was retelling the incident in detail the next time our Dad came to visit us, he asked her where they'd taken Mr. Twelve-Foot-Long Python. "Back to the wild," she answered.

"Not much different from our garden," he mumbled. "Snake Paradise."

A crew arrived the morning after to see whether any other members of the family had been left behind, but they didn't find any. The most amazing thing was that what was clearly an emergency was dismissed as a mere incident right after it happened, then hushed up for good. As much as I try to make sense of the way my Humans view things, it's not easy. I mean, puh-leeze. We're talking about a twelve-foot-long python that had been living beside the pond right in front of our porch and probably slithering around in our house every time we went out!

The only reason I could think of for keeping the whole thing quiet was so it wouldn't scare off their friends who were coming to stay with us at Christmas, and I guess once you've stooped to a cover-up, you're more or less committed for life. They held true to their commitment. The incident was never mentioned again.

* * *

Aside from that day, I can think of only one other time during our breezy life in Chiangmai when we broke the number one rule and didn't smile. It was our run-in with the Rottweiler, and trust me, there was nothing to smile about.

We'd had some quality wake-up time upstairs on our bed with our Dad, who was home again from Vietnam, and set out immediately afterward for our run with our Mom. We were halfway to the gate that took us out and along the *klongs,* when she looked up and saw the Rottweiler standing halfway down the block in the middle of the road. She immediately ran us into a neighbor's garden and yelled for help, holding on to our leashes for dear life, but nobody heard and nobody came. And then he was on us.

My memory is a blurred jumble of the rough, guttural sounds and ferocious snarls that came from deep down in his throat, his low growls and wet, sloppy snorts; of Brie's trembling little body beside mine and my Mom butting up against him, trying to fend him off with her knee; of the sudden impact of his huge mass of quivering muscle coming down on top of me with full force; of a piercing pain shooting through my chest, then my leg; of Brie squirming and thrashing underneath; and finally, of the dead weight of him lumbering off of us.

We stayed exactly where he left us: face down on the wet grass, almost too afraid to breathe, listening to his labored panting inches away and picking up the foul smell of him. Minutes without movement—only the coarse sound of his hot, heavy breath. Finally, a splutter as he shook himself off, then a rough, gravelly noise as though he was pawing at something, more thick, raspy wheezes and the grating sound again, farther away this time. He was on the driveway, distancing himself.

Still, we lay there motionless, our hearts pounding, our eyes peeking out through damp, matted fur, listening for a trace of him but hearing only our own shaky gasps for air. Brie looked very small and frightened, but she was unharmed—I think because she was tangled up somewhere in the middle of it all. Our Mom was beside us, clutching our leads, and I could see cuts and scratches on her thigh and deep lines across her face. She hadn't moved a muscle or spoken a word since he'd left; she just stood there, staring out guardedly toward the road, taking long, slow breaths, waiting until she was sure he was gone. At long last, she knelt down, put her arms around both of us and buried her head in our fur, and then ever so slowly helped us to our feet.

I don't know why he left us there in a disheveled heap. Maybe he felt he'd done what he'd set out to do, but we didn't care. It was over—no more than a sliver in time, and we were alive. When we limped through our gate, we were one sorry sight. My Mom relayed a quick version of what had happened to my Dad as he carried me to the car then drove to the vet at record-breaking speed. As soon as we were inside, I was lifted up onto a cold table and given some jabs on my neck and leg.

My Mom and Dad sat on stools beside me gently massaging my back, speaking in soft, comforting tones. I vaguely remember the doctor cutting my fur but nothing else. The next thing I knew, I was on the carpet in our front hall, with Brie lying next to me, the silky feel of her against my side. She stayed there all night, and every so often, she lifted her head and licked the spots where my bandages were.

There was a lot of talk between my Mom and Dad and our neighbors afterward, but it was mostly Human mumbo jumbo that I couldn't understand.

"The owner should … blah … (?!!?) blah, blah."

"Someone should … blah … (?!!?) … blah PO-LEECE!"

"Anywhere else, that dawg … (?!!?)!"[9]

We never saw the Rottweiler again, but he came back to haunt me in my dreams, and the memory of him stayed with me for a long time. The nightmares were always the same. I'd hear his deep growls and thick, gruff snarls and look up to see him charging toward me, his enormous chest heaving, his mouth wide open, baring his jagged teeth, the full mass of him leaping into the air—then, everything would turn black.

---

9 The owner paid the police, so nothing was done. Harry had fifteen stitches in his leg and twenty-two in his chest. Later, the same dog attacked a child. Again, no action was taken.

It was my own cries and whimpers that brought me crashing back to reality; in fact, for a while I had to stop my regular 2:00 p.m. zzzzzzzzs altogether, for fear he'd be on me the second I dozed off. To my great relief, I discovered a way to get my life back on track, and if you happen to be one of the less fortunate who have had a run-in with a Rottweiler, or some other vicious breed, I strongly suggest you try it; otherwise, you could be plagued with those nightmares for the rest of your life. It's a step-by-step process and completely fail-safe.

Step One: The next time you're catapulted out of a terrifying dream and brought back to that bewildering state of reality vs. unreality, the first thing you do is check your surroundings.

Nine out of ten times guaranteed, you'll find yourself sprawled out in one of your favorite snoozing spots, which will vary depending on the time of year and your mood.

Because there are only two seasons in Ho Chi Minh City, both of which require cover, Brie and I are never very hard to find. During Hot and Hotter, we're in one of our freshly sculpted trenches in the garden, on the floor of the upstairs verandah or in the shower off the guest bedroom. During Wet and Wetter, we stick to the verandah or the bathroom, unless there's a thunderstorm, in which case we immediately retreat to the crawl space under our Mom's computer.

Step Two: After you've determined your territory's not the least bit hostile, assume one of your best downward-facing dawg poses of all time, pressing your front paws to the ground, squeezing your shoulder blades together, keeping your rear end high and making sure your head doesn't droop. Hold the stretch until you feel the tension in every muscle of your body, then stand up and give yourself a long, rigorous shake.

Step Three: Feeling absolutely confident that you're back in real time, will your nightmare to exit your subconscious forever. I know, it sounds totally far-fetched, and what's probably going through your brain is, "Right, Harry, easy for you, Eastern Mantra Yoga Dawg," but I promise, it works. All you have to do is close your eyes, focus and come as close as you can to barking *Om mani padme hum,* my

Mom's mantra—*same same* "the jewel in the lotus" (?!!?)—two or three times. It's a simple case of mind over matter.

Step Four: Reconstruct the ending so that you come out looking a lot better than I did on the doctor's table in Chiangmai, and you'll be cured forever. The last time I saw that Rottweiler in a dream, the bell had sounded and I was being paraded around the ring as if I was Muhammad Ali himself, a red-and-gold satin cape draped over my shoulders, my right paw raised in victory to the thunderous roar of the crowd, the lights on the scoreboard flashing repeatedly: Harry, 2 ... Rottweiler, zip!

Right after my stitches came out, my Dad came to Chiangmai to take us all to Ho Chi Minh City. As sad as we felt about leaving Ohmsin and Tui and all our other VBFs in Chiangmai, there'd be no more anxious waiting for our Dad to come and see us or heart-wrenching good-byes when he left. We were going to be a family again, like we're meant to be, and it can't get much better than that. Our layover in Chiangmai could possibly have been the longest layover in aviation history!

CHAPTER 9
Ho Chi Minh City

The thing Brie and I missed most after leaving Chiangmai was going everywhere in our Mom's car. A car is pretty much out of the question in Ho Chi Minh City, because we live in the heart of Chaos Central, and a lot of money would have to go to the PO-LEECE if we had an accident. It would always be our fault, too, which doesn't seem fair, but our Dad says, "It doesn't have to be because we're *người nước ngoài*," ("Humans living outside their country"). So we're living a car-free life, with an occasional taxi ride to the vet or a trip in a van to the beach, which is one of the best exceptions to our routine that we can hope for!

We live across the Sông Sài Gòn Bridge in the district of An Phú, away from the crowded city streets, the unbroken sound of horns and the *xe môtô* (motorbike) madness. Even though it was my Dad who found our house, it has presented an extremely annoying problem for him for which there appears to be no apparent solution. It's the old taxi driver dilemma and the pronunciation of An Phú, which he's expected to sing in the right key to be understood and get himself home at the end of the day. I think he's getting better in terms of removing himself from the first taxi and flagging down another before the situation deteriorates, but the whole process is far more complicated than

he would like. Despite the difficulties, he has had no regrets in choosing our beautiful house and garden in An Phú.

If you were to conjure up the perfect garden in your mind, ours has everything you would imagine and more. It's a canine's dream come true, with trees and bushes and beautiful shady spots to while away long afternoons, a tiled area where our Mom and Dad have their coffee in the mornings and Brie and I practice skim boarding on our paws, deep flower beds for digging perfectly sculpted trenches to lie in during the dawg days of summer, pomegranate and mango trees with enough fruit for everyone in our neighborhood, hibiscus plants crying out for our attention, white-flowered bushes with such heavenly smells they make us giddy and goofy at the same time, and lots of room to run with soft green grass underfoot.

There's even a dog lap pool that used to be a fish tank when our house was an Irish pub. The odd Human expat, who knew it before, sometimes rings the bell and asks if we're open. Usually we're not, but sometimes when our Mom and Dad aren't doing much they'll ask them in for a beer. Brie's in and out of the lap pool umpteen times a day when she's having her manic outbursts, and in between, she stands on one spot to keep cool.

We have a real swimming pool as well that we swam in when we first got here, with our Mom and Dad watching us, but it was declared "Off Limits," and they had a fence put up around it. The only way out is up the ladder, which would be much too steep a learning curve for us. We actually know a dawg named Lupa, whose Humans taught her how to do it, but she's got much daintier paws than we do. Whoops, they left the gate open!

Brie had her gecko patrols up and running within a few days, combing the house to check out her best surveillance points. The geckos are

bigger and noisier here than they were in Hanoi and Chiangmai, which makes them easier to spot and seems to have heightened her curiosity. The bright-green ones with blue on their legs are her prize catches.

When we're inside at night, we sit out on the upstairs verandah, which is the most ree-laxed part of our house, with fans for us to snooze under during the day and a table where our Mom and Dad eat most nights, except during *mùa mưa,* when the wind whips the blinds around and the rain comes in. On clear nights, we can see the stars twinkling, and sometimes there's a moon as round as a dinner plate that lights up the whole sky. When we go to bed, it peeps through the window and throws light on all of us.

It's as if the whole setup was especially chosen for Brie and me, with everything our hearts could desire right at our paws. Out the gate, down the lane to the big road, a good run at a nice easy pace and we're at our own private beach on the Sông Sài Gòn, with a ramp to jump off when the river's high and a beach to explore when the tide's low. Our latest and biggest discovery has been coconuts, which have to be one of the coolest things in the entire world.

I think their instant appeal came from our love of tennis balls and the phenomenal number of things the two have in common. You're

probably thinking, "Come on, Harry, that's so far-fetched," which is exactly my point. They're perfect for fetching on land or in water, though water is preferable in Ho Chi Minh City on account of how many end up on our beach, which by the way, my Dad has renamed "Coconut Landing."

The other similarity is they're ideal for shredding; in fact, I use the same technique I do for shredding tennis balls, so it's a totally transferable skill. All you have to do is position yourself directly over the coconut, making sure it's tightly secured between your paws, get a good grip on the pulp, clench your teeth as hard as you can and pull straight up using short, quick tugs. It's not like we've abandoned our tennis balls; it's just that there's room in our lives for both.

Our garden is teeming with lowlife 24/7, especially frogs, which I don't think will hurt us as long as they're not poison darts. Occasionally, we chase them, but I'm not sure what we'd do if we caught one. Our Mom had an unexpected frog incident the other morning that my Dad found very funny, even though she didn't. She was sitting outside putting her running shoes on when she suddenly let out a high-pitched squeal—not as loud as the one she let out last week when she saw a bat coming at her from the light in the spare bedroom, mind you, but it was still a squeal.

The frog in the shoe was so minor in comparison that it can't be called anything other than a "Nike Moment." It was just a baby frog looking for a place to hide, and as soon as it felt her foot, it leapt out of the shoe and was gone, probably scared to death. My Dad finally got her to laugh, but it wasn't her normal laugh, and I could tell she didn't think it was funny, even though she'll eventually tell it as though it was.

Her reactions vary a lot depending on the day, and sometimes all it takes is an encounter with a lowlife like a baby frog to send her over the edge. It's not that tiny little creature itself that sets her off; it's that she's reached a kind of breaking point where she longs for things to be almost a little bit boring, like they used to be, before

we landed in terra incognita. Something suddenly stirs up thoughts of our other house and the neighborhood we used to live in, with its pristine garden and peace and quiet—no horns honking at nothing, no streets teeming

with motorbikes that she's afraid to cross, no Dawg Mafia wanting to grab us, PO-LEECE who are there to help, not to take what they can, water that's clear and clean, parks and long stretches of beach where we can run off lead, friends like Griffey and Max and Riley, family like Big Joe and Sara and Captain Crunch—everything that used to be normal.

I don't know how I forgot to mention this earlier, because it's another very predictable part of culture shock. It can come right after the gobsmacked stage, along with the meltdowns and outbursts, or much later, out of nowhere, when they think they're doing fine, and suddenly they're not. They're miles away, in the same places Brie and I go in our dreams; they're home, at least in their hearts and their minds, and they're aching inside. The feeling comes and goes with tears and a heavy heart, even after years of being *người nước ngoài*. There's no remedy for it, and it goes away in its own time. It's homesickness.

* * *

Now the no-mad cows are normal, and the rat she discovered on the front burner of the stove, the lizards and snakes, the frog in her shoe and the mayhem as soon as she steps out the gate. Like I said, her mood depends on the day. Some days she's as carefree as can be, and sometimes when she goes back to Canada she even misses the color of chaos. Go figure!

For some reason, I feel far more ree-laxed in Ho Chi Minh City than I did in Hanoi. I think it's because we don't have to worry about the Dawg Mafia as much. My Dad says "it's mostly a northern thing, but we still have to be careful, especially around Tet." We haven't had a single accident since we've been here, we didn't have to put in all those long hours waiting for inspection, nor were we gawked at like animals in a zoo.

We go everywhere with our Mom and Dad, and we can even walk to the An Phú supermarket and wait outside like I used to do in Hong

Kong. They still don't take us to restaurants with "exotic dishes and chickens running around," but we're allowed to sit with our Mom when she has coffee at the roadside shop near our house. That's Minh, who lives with us and is our NVBF in Ho Chi Minh City, with one of our Mom's new VBFs, Priscilla.

There are these walled places called "compounds" near our house where a lot of Human expats live, and we see quite a few Goldens when we go there. The biggest compound is called BP. My Dad says "it's a lot like this place called Pleasantville" (?!!?), because "once you get inside, all the streets look the same and it's almost impossible to find someone's house." When we go to Jessie's, we have to look

for special numbers, and if we can't find them, we just go home. Jessie's a Cocker Spaniel and our only real canine friend here. We have play dates with her when we can find her house, and when her Humans go away she comes to stay with us. Our Mom's trying to teach her not to jump up by shaking a beer can full of coins, but it's not really working. Jessie's pretty much her own person, if you know what I mean—kind of zany like Brie. That's Brie barking at a conical hat.

Our street is mostly local shop houses with very few

real houses, so it's far less confusing than BP, with just the Brahma bulls meandering by and the potbelly pig hanging out beside the barber's shop. The other day, we saw him fall off a wagon and go squealing down the street with a whole bunch of people chasing him, which was kind of odd since he doesn't normally do much  of anything except sleep and roll around in the mud. I don't have a clue what he was doing in the wagon in the first place.

Something else I don't understand is why my Dad calls the barber's shop a shop. I mean, all the barber does is hang a mirror on the wall across the road from our house, drag out an old chair from the empty lot in behind and wait for his first customer to walk in the door. Excuse me—what door?

My Dad thinks it's "cool" not having "any overhead," but it's not. It's hotter than you can imagine, except during *mùa mưa,* and who wants to get their hair cut in the pouring rain? On a slow day, he just lies around on the hammock beside his shop (NOT!) while the pig sleeps underneath, snorting like crazy.

What was definitely cool was Hu`ng, a friend of my Mom and Dads, arriving early one morning in his van to drive us to Long Hai beach. Of course, we had no way of knowing we were going to the beach, but we knew we were going somewhere new, not just to the vet in a taxi.

The day was sunny and Brie and I were as happy as we could stand it, zooming around the garden in circles until we were so dizzy we had to flop down on the grass to get our bearings. Minh, Hu`ng and our Mom and Dad were loading the van, and let me tell you, what was going in looked pretty promising. My Dad had just put a carton

in the back seat with not one but two brand-new tins of Dunlops, our orange Chuckit with its superhuman capacity to send our tennis balls to the Outer Limits, a stack of old towels for independent or coopera-tive play and our extra-long leashes. Hu`ng and Minh had loaded two coolers, a small bag of Science Diet, and our snack packs and bowls, and our Mom was coming out of the house with some soft bags and bottles of whatever it is they drink when my Dad comes home from work. Sometimes it's red and sometimes it's white (!??!). WHOA! This was no routine outing.

Once we hit the road, we couldn't have been more content, cruising down the highway, taking in the green fields, the long, straight rows of trees and the silvery salt fields shimmering in the morning light with Hu`ng, our Mom and Dad, and music for the open road. We don't ever worry about how long it will take to get somewhere: twenty-seven seconds, twenty-seven hours, fifty-nine minutes—it doesn't matter as long as we get there eventually. Having said that, this is probably as good a time as any to tell you a little about "our time," which isn't nearly as complicated for us as it is for our Humans, who spend half their lives checking the gazillion clocks and watches they

have outside their bodies so that they can get someplace on time but never do.

Our clocks, on the other hand, are inside our bodies, and because our days are pretty ree-laxed and not totally wild and frantic like theirs, we don't have to check them constantly; in fact, we don't have to check them at all. They check us, and they keep perfect time without ever being slow and making us miss something really important, like an airplane, which is what my Mom and Dad's clocks made them do in Hong Kong.

There they were, just lollygagging around, going back and forth between the kitchen and our bedroom, getting more coffee, sitting down on the bed to listen to the man on TV talk about "Hong Kong going back to China," sauntering over to look for some socks or a baseball cap every once in a while and dropping them into their suitcases nonchalantly, as if they had all the time in the world until— Whoops! The man on TV said, "The time here in Hong Kong is blah, blah, blah" (?!!?), which must have been completely different from what their clocks said because WOW! did they ever pick up the pace.

Suddenly, they were flying around like chickens with their heads cut off, grabbing papers and Dawg knows what to put in their suitcases; changing their minds, taking something out and throwing something else in; running to the bathroom and rushing out a few minutes later with armfuls of little ziplocks filled with tubes and cans and jars, stuffing them into their cases then bouncing on top of them to try to get them closed; and spurting shrill mumbo jumbo as they ran out to the taxi, dragging their coats and jackets behind them, jumped in, slammed the door and took off, waving their arms madly out the windows until they were out of sight. You had to see it to believe it!

I moseyed into the kitchen and lay down next to the stove to get a little peace and quiet after their spectacular performance and had no sooner stretched out on the floor with my head on one paw just the way I like it, when I heard a car. The door opened and in they came, shoulders slumped, heads hanging almost down to the floor, looking completely despondent. As my Mom toddled past, she gave me a small pat on the head, then disappeared into the bedroom. It never happened again.

We don't bother with the split seconds, minutes and hours our Humans are always fussing about. Our time blocks are much bigger and come from the knowing feeling we get inside our tummies, the sun's position in the sky and the long morning and afternoon shadows in our garden. These tell us everything we need to know.

Because our schedule is pretty much the same every day, we can tell immediately if there's a change, and this part isn't complicated either, seeing as there are very few changes. Hu`ng's van appearing in our driveway to take us to the beach is a good example of an exception. Another would be our kennels showing up in the kitchen, our lives being turned upside down as soon as the truck arrives and spending endless hours in Deep Dark Cargo. I don't think I've mentioned this invisible line you cross when you're flying across the pond, which is so beyond weird it's hard to even think about. I mean, how can you cross a line that isn't there? But you do, and your inside clock gets so scrambled you don't have a clue whether it's breakfast or dinner, not to mention what you're supposed to be doing "in between." *Excusez moi?* In between what and what?

Anyway, back to our concept of time. Our main sub-blocks come in twos, namely breakfast and dinner, and everything else falls effortlessly in between. It's important to know that these two sub-blocks are the absolute hub of our existence from which all else flows. You'll get the picture when I go through a typical day:

Wake-up time:

We always wake up earlier than our Mom and Dad, but we've learned to lie there and wait until our inside clock tells us it's 7:00 a.m. We don't actually know it's 7:00 a.m. like our Humans do, but according to our Mom and Dad, who check their clocks, their watches, their mobile phones, the TV and the computer, it always is. We get up off the carpet and amble around to the side of their bed to give them each a nudge. I guess you could also call this part of our day "nudge time." They respond with groggy pats, and we go back to our places on the carpet.

7:25 a.m.:

Our inside alarm goes off, letting us know it's time to thunder down the stairs for early outside time, when we attend to our business and futz around the garden for a while, sniffing the little flowers that make us goofy and harassing the lowlife before going in the side door to the kitchen to hang around and wait for breakfast.

8:00 a.m.:

If breakfast is on time, we're usually finished by 8:03 at the latest. We wait for our water and have a long, sloppy drink, then charge out the kitchen door and chase each other around the garden, back through the kitchen and dining room, and out the front door two or three times at optimum speed.

8:06 a.m. to 8:30 a.m.:

Time to careen across the tiles and screech to a halt to spend quality time with our Dad, either on the table or beside it, while he has his coffee and fruit. We get two pieces of fruit each—usually mango, papaya, pineapple, pomelo or watermelon. Once in a while, there'll be something different, like *vú sũa* (mother's milk), which sounds exotic but is just plain old star apple, so don't let it fool you. None of this is our choice, mind you, seeing as our Dad's the one who divvies up the fruit, but we're always grateful for his generosity. The 8:06 to 8:30 slot is also a ree-lax time until our Mom saddles us up for our run.

8:30 a.m. to (?!!?):

Run and possible swim at the Sông Sài Gòn, though the swim isn't guaranteed when it's just my Mom. Coffee at a shop house and sometimes more coffee at another Human expat's. If there's another dawg, like Jessie, it's called a play date.

10:30 a.m. on:

Futzing around in the garden again, checking out the lowlife and flower beds and digging fresh trenches for our naps; standing in the wading pool peering woefully through the fence at the Off Limits Human pool; wandering through the house to see if anything's changed; sniffing around in the kitchen in case there's something cooking or left where it shouldn't be; followed by our morning snooze, which usually runs into the hottest part of the day. We wake up briefly, stretch, then reposition ourselves and settle in for our afternoon nap. This whole part of the day is downtime, unless one of those signals goes off in our brains, telling us something's happening downstairs or outside.

The signal can be as subtle as our Mom opening the cupboard where she keeps the peanut butter, soup simmering on the stove or a new lowlife arriving in the house or garden. But it can also be as jarring as the rude awakening from the rooster next door, who has no idea how to tell the time, or the sharp, muddled jabber that comes with the daily kerfuffles outside our gate. We try not to let these disruptions ruin our naps, but occasionally they do.

4:30 p.m.:

Wake-up time, when the sun is lower in the sky and we sense the Brahma bull is passing on his way to the pool hall. This is usually the same time as our afternoon outing, when we either follow the bull up the road to the turnoff and wait while our Mom goes into a shop house or go down to the river to watch the colors fading in and out and the crimson glow making its way across the sky before it gets dark.

6:30 p.m.:

Dinner followed by a drink and another mad chase around the

garden, back through the kitchen and dining room and out the front door—two laps minimum, more if time permits.

6:34 p.m.:

Gate duty waiting for our Dad, which can be long or short, depending on the taxi driver dilemma that day. Sometimes, we do a little sniffing around the garden to keep from getting bored, but we're always super alert, listening beyond the wall for the sound of the motor so that we don't disappoint him when he comes through the gate.

7:30 p.m.:

Nightly greeting with our Dad. The taxi pulls up, we hear the door open and close, the gate opens and we watch our Dad's face light up the minute he sees us. He crouches down and draws us both into him, burying his head between us and scratching our ears. We look up at him and for a brief moment we're almost completely still, our eyes alight, locked intently into his, but it's impossible to contain our excitement for very long. Behinds wiggling, tails wagging and whipping back and forth, faces hopelessly happy, we start jumping, leaping and prancing beside him as we make our way up the path to the house. Triple love and joy.

7:35 p.m.:

Upstairs while they have a glass of something and my Mom runs through any incidents that happened that day. More yakking, then a time-out to watch Brie on her gecko patrol. Await arrival of food on the table and stay in close range while they eat dinner in case of spillage, listening to laughter or grave voices as they go through the events of the day.

8:30 p.m.:

Downstairs for kitchen duty (i.e., plate cleaning), which can be short or long, depending on volume and stickage.

8:45 p.m.:

Out into the garden and the cool night air. Our Mom and Dad usually sit on the front steps, talking quietly and watching us while we do our separate investigations, disappearing into the bushes before the inevitable moment when we reappear, plunk ourselves down facing one another and pause, priming ourselves for one last mad tear around the garden. Panting happily, we follow our Mom and Dad inside. This time slot can be cut short if the bats are swooping too close to the front porch.

9:10 p.m.:

A nice long drink and cool-down before our Mom and Dad finish their chat or read the paper. This can be in the kitchen, unless there's a sticky square on the counter to catch rats—one in particular has been making frequent appearances—the upstairs living room if it's *mùa mưa* or outside on the verandah, our area of choice.

Last event of the day:

Into our bedroom to watch CNN, Discovery Channel and/or a DVD they put on almost every night. I know the man in the DVD's name is Jack, because it's the same as a dawg who comes to Jessie's house for play dates sometimes, except this Jack spends his whole life either yelling "NOW" into his cell phone or on a wild car chase. Then there's this lady who's always clicking away on her computer and shouting at Jack to get back to CTU (!??!). After they've been watching it for a while, the picture "breaks up" and there's nothing but bright pink and green fluorescent squares on the screen. My Dad says he'll "pick up another DVD at the Russian market tomorrow," but it's never any different. The next night, Jack's in this enormous plane with no one driving it, cutting all these different colored wires. There's a ticking sound like a clock, the fluorescent squares come back and they groan and turn off the TV.

Lights out, hearts full after a perfect day, we float off into dreams of tennis balls, coconuts, geckos, long runs, the beach at Long Hai, baguettes and our Mom and Dad. High hopes and promises for tomorrow.

Since our Mom started teaching every day, there's been a noticeable change in our routine. Morning runs have been moved to a new slot at the crack of dawn when we're still half asleep. She keeps apologizing but says we'll "get used to it." Minh takes her to school on his motorbike afterward, which makes our early mosey around the garden slightly longer than before. Breakfast, speed laps, skim boarding across the tiles and quality time with our Dad are unchanged, thank Dawg!

And that's our schedule in a nutshell and how time works for us, so I think you'll understand now why we had no idea how long it took us to get to Long Hai. But we did get there; in fact, Hư`ng had just turned off the main road and driven to the top of a steep driveway. We'd arrived at our first ever hotel in Vietnam, or Thailand for that matter!

The only other hotel Brie and I had ever stayed in together was a "park your paws, bed & biscuit" sort of place in Canada when our Mom and Dad went away somewhere. You could choose a single, luxury or deluxe room. Our Mom and Dad chose the luxury, which was also called a condominium in the paper they were given to read. My Dad said it was "deceptive advertising because condominiums usually have an upstairs" (?!!?). Anyway, it was big enough for two and better than being crammed into a single. The deluxe room had classical music and a special "Wag-tail bed," whatever that means. When our Mom checked whether we could bring some of our personal things, like our own blankets and a few toys, the lady said it was okay, which was a huge relief, because the first place they checked said, "Absolutely not!"

There was a fenced-in area we could play in every day, and your Humans had to choose different things for you to do. Ours chose the Two Play Group A Day over the All-Day Pass, to get a discount. If you stayed more than seven days, you got a free bath and a certificate when you left, but we weren't there long enough.

The only thing missing was a place to swim, but we really didn't have any complaints. I think it was probably a three star hotel. Our schedule was stricter than at home, with walks for all the "guests" (which is what they called us when they gave our Mom and Dad the tour), before breakfast when we were still groggy, after our first snooze and when the sun was starting to go down. We were taken for a special walk when we checked in to "put us at ease" before we went to our room. My Mom and Dad laughed so hard when they heard that one, they were almost rolling on the floor.

The paper they got said "friendly, caring staff 24/7," which was mostly true, except for one grouchy lady who I figured was just fed up with the whole thing. All things considered, we had a pretty good time but were over the moon to get home, which you always are after a holiday, especially without your Humans. Bedtime without our Mom and Dad was especially hard, and even during the day we had a few bouts of homesickness, though I think we caught it from the dawg next door. Whenever he started howling, someone would come and stay with him and the next thing I knew, I was wailing just like him and Brie was copying me. One of the attendants came and brought us each a milk bone, so we kept on being homesick for the next few days.

Before we went to Hong Kong and then adopted Brie, I stayed in a few other hotels when I went on a road trip with my Mom and Dad, which is one of the coolest things you can do. You just cruise down the open road with your head out the window and your ears flapping like crazy, stopping at all these different places along the way. When the sky starts turning bright shades of red and pink, you drive slower until you find someplace to sleep. We spent a few nights at a cowboy hotel, and after breakfast, we went for a hike and found a spot near a beautiful mountain stream to have lunch. The water was ice cold, and when I lay in it, I could feel

all the smooth stones under my tummy, which was incredibly sooth-ing. I was allowed in the restaurant, and no one kicked up a fuss like they do in Ho Chi Minh City, but there weren't any live chickens. Everyone patted me, and by the time my Mom and Dad had finished eating the first night, I'd made four NVBFs—all cowboys. My Mom and Dad were the only ones in the hotel who weren't wearing cowboy boots and hats, but no one seemed to care. I was so full of happiness on that road trip, I could hardly sit still, and the trip to Long Hai was exactly the same.

The hotel was called Anoasis. After Hu`ng parked the car, we walked up some steps to meet some Humans and check in, then we went down a walkway to our little house overlooking the sea. Directly in front was a path that led up to the dining room and another that went to the beach. We had room service while our Mom and Dad went up the hill for dinner. Otherwise, we were together from mor-ning till night.

The first thing we saw after we checked out our little house was a butterfly lizard lying completely still at the bottom of the steps with his body in a perfect cobra pose. My Dad said he was "a legend at lunchtime," which I didn't really understand. Brie took a good long look but didn't bother him. The sound of the waves was much more intriguing to her.

We took off down the path and in a heartbeat were running the full length of the beach, bounding in and out of the water, playing in the surf and digging our way to China. Brie had never been to a real

beach before, and it was like being right inside the Discovery Channel, with sea turtles and sand crabs everywhere. We watched in awe as these tiny little creatures burrowed into the sand, then popped out and skittered off down the

beach. Sultry sea breezes swished past our noses, and frothy white waves carried us on their crests. It was so bright, we had to close our eyes to get used to it, and the sand was so hot beneath our paws, we had to skip and jump to the water's edge.

Sometimes, we were so completely overcome with joy that we just stood on the beach barking at the waves crashing in to shore. At the end of the day, we sat with our Mom and Dad and watched the sun send sheets of red across the sky before dropping into the sea like a huge fiery ball.

By dinnertime, that dawg-tiredness had caught up with us, and when our Mom and Dad went up for dinner, we were already curled up on the bamboo porch outside. We lay there for a long time, our eyes glazing over but our senses wide awake, breathing in the salty sea air, listening to the calming sound of the water and the cicadas buzzing in the trees. The butterfly lizard was still at the bottom of the stairs, watching over us like a sentry.

We were awakened bright and early the next morning by the same sights, smells and sounds of the day before—a clear, cloudless sky as blue as the sea, fresh air and gentle breezes brushing against our faces, and the water shimmering in the bright sunshine washing the sand white as it moved toward the shore. Our day was spent riding the waves, chasing crabs down the beach, running after our tennis balls and wagging eternal gratitude to our Mom and Dad. When it was time to go, we settled comfortably into the back seat of the van, our hearts so full of happiness there wasn't room for anything else. There didn't need to be.

CHAPTER 10
After Long Hai

My memories of the sequence of events in our lives over the next days and months are hazy in places, but I do know that sometime after our weekend at the beach, Brie started favoring one leg—not all the time but often enough for us to notice.

I could see my Mom and Dad were worried. They took her to a new vet they'd heard about near the airport, so we got to go for quite a few taxi rides. Brie would stand up in the back seat and lean over the taxi driver's shoulder, scaring him half to death, and my Mom would laugh and pull her back. My Dad would often meet us there after work, and there would be long, quiet conversations after Brie had seen the doctor. Then we'd go home with medicine for her leg.

The vet said she needed to have something called "an X-ray," but there wasn't a special place for dawg X-rays in Ho Chi Minh City, so we had to go to a Human one. It was a dark, dingy shop house, and as soon as we were inside, Brie was lifted up onto a cold metal table where she had to lie very still. It wasn't easy for her, but she tried hard and managed with my Mom and Dad's help. Finally, the X-ray man said "BLie finish—Go!" and we left with a big brown envelope full of pictures of Brie's leg. On the way home, my Dad said he was "going to send them through the computer."

How he got those enormous pictures to make their way to our vet in Canada through the computer will always be a mystery to me, but I know they did get there, because the vet called the very next morning. We were all upstairs when the phone rang, and my Mom and Dad held it between them so that they could both listen. It seemed to take a long time for his words to register, but when they did, a deep sadness fell over the room, and from then on, it followed them wherever they went. The doctor's voice had reached through the phone and handed them the truth. There was something terribly wrong with Brie.

The next day, we went to the Vietnamese vet again, with Brie standing up in the back seat, just like always, leaning way over the taxi driver's shoulder, grinning from ear to ear. The vet was going to give her a test. Minh came with us so that he could talk to the doctor, and when they came out of the back with Brie, jabbering away in their singsongy voices, they were both smiling.

"BLie okay! BLie better—operation later," the doctor said. This sounded like very good news to me, and we drove home with more medicine, though for some reason, my Mom and Dad didn't seem happy or convinced. When they sent the picture from the test to our vet in Canada, he told them "there was nothing on it." He also told them that Brie couldn't have an operation, which was not what the Vietnamese doctor had said. So they stopped believing in her, and we never went back.

Someone had told them about a new French vet who had just arrived in Ho Chi Minh City, and they arranged for him to come to the house. He eyes were soft brown and his face was open and kind, like Dr. Die's in Hanoi. When he laid his hands on Brie, she seemed to relax immediately, and he instilled trust and confidence in my Mom and Dad. After his first visit, he came regularly to give Brie medicine, and she was always better afterward. We started playing in the garden again and going for walks, and she even did her gecko patrols, except she didn't jump anymore; she would just sit patiently looking

up, waiting for the gecko to drop. Worry turned to hope, and for a small window of time, our house was full of joy and life went back to what it had been before Brie got sick.

The big change came around the same time that Santa Claus arrived in Ho Chi Minh City, because I remember we'd been for a walk on the main road near the river and had seen all the Santas riding past on their motorbikes. Brie and I had done a double-take as they roared by in their fluffy red Santa suits with their long, white beards, waving and smiling and having the time of their lives. It was Brie's last outing.

Suddenly, a dark cloud closed in around us. The French vet started coming every day to give Brie medicine or a needle, and she'd bounce back for brief periods, but her good days became fewer and fewer. My Mom and Dad would sit quietly, holding her head in their laps, patting and stroking her for long stretches while I'd lie at their feet. When it was time for bed, they'd carry her upstairs and lay her down gently. I'd settle in right next to her and stay there till morning, feeling the soft silkiness of her beside me.

Sara was coming to visit for Christmas, and the day after she arrived, Brie didn't get up off the floor. She just lay there, almost motionless, sleeping. Every once in a while, her eyes would open for a split second, then glaze over, and she'd sleep some more. The doctor came and gave her another needle, and Sara and my Mom sat on the carpet with her all day, leaving only to get more ice cubes for her to suck or a fresh cold pack to put on her forehead. Later, they took her to the upstairs bathroom and laid her down on the cool tiles. They stayed with her all night, never leaving her side, their hands or their heads against her, speaking in quiet, soothing voices, comforting and reassuring her.

I went into my Mom and Dad's room and slept on my usual spot at the end of their bed. When I woke up the next morning and walked through the hall to the bathroom, the sun's rays were streaming in the window and they were still there. My Mom took me downstairs, then got on the phone. She was crying, and although I couldn't understand most of what she was saying, I knew she was talking to my Dad. "Please, Michael" (?!!?) she said. "Tell the doctor to" (?!!?). She had just hung up the phone when Sara called from upstairs. "Mom, he doesn't need to tell the vet to come. She's gone. She did it on her own."

We ran upstairs, and my Mom sat on the floor, then laid her hand next to Sara's on Brie's back. Her little body was so still. Tears streamed down their faces, and they stroked her and told her how much they loved her and would miss her. As I lay there next to her, I felt a heaviness in my heart I can't begin to describe. It was as if it was breaking into a million pieces. We stayed there, barely moving, waiting for my Dad to come home, and when he did, he sat with her for a long time, speaking softly, then buried his head in her fur and wept.

Jessie's Mom came with her friend Mr. Tam in his van and my

Dad and Minh wrapped Brie in her blue blanket, carried her outside and laid her gently in the back seat. We all got in and drove until we reached the green, away from the city, and after a while, we turned onto a narrow road that ended at the bottom of a hill. Steep steps led us partway up to a path that wound its way through the forest.

We hadn't gone very far when we came to a beautiful spot where the sun was streaming through the trees and the ground was soft. It was here where we laid Brie to rest. Her

body went back to Mother Earth, with her blanket, her blue squeaky ball, a tennis ball and a little silver Buddha. A monk in his orange robe came down from the pagoda on the hill, spoke a few words, nodded gently and left.

When we got home, Sara and my Mom and I sat quietly on the front porch feeling the overwhelming sadness in Brie's absence. A few days later, my Dad read a poem he'd written for Brie that afternoon, and the most amazing thing happened while he was reading it. A little gecko appeared out of nowhere and ran across his bare foot. We all saw it. It was as though "happiness had snuck in a door we didn't know was left open." Brie was already up to her old tricks!

> Brie
> Like the wind she ran through our lives,
> Evoking supreme joy in the simple pleasures of running,
>   leaping and swimming.
> She was a performing artist.
> No stage needed,
> She performed wherever she happened to find herself with
>   her props of tennis balls, towels and squeaky toys backed
>   up by her perpetual grin.
> She earned many sobriquets—
> "Little Girl," "Little Princess," "Sweetness and Light,"
> And responded equally to all of them.
> She took all life on—
> Humans, roosters, chickens, geckos, all scrutinized.
> She backed away from nothing
> And when the stranger in the night came with the offer
> that she was unable to refuse,
> She showed for one last time that nothing,
> Not even death, could best her spirit,
> Could best our little Breezie.

Even though I knew deep down she was gone, I wandered everywhere looking for her. Her pink kennel sat in one corner of the kitchen and her scent drifted through the air, inside and out. I could see her with her feet planted firmly on the ground and her head cocked to one side, pleading with me with her soft, innocent eyes to come and play. "Puh-leeze, Har-eee … Puh-leeze," they'd say. "You know how much I love you."

When they knew I was feeling especially sad, my Mom and Dad would sit with me between them and speak quietly. "Don't worry, Harry," they'd say. "We promise she's all right. You have to trust us on this." And ever so slowly, it became easier. I filled the special place in my heart I keep for dreams with the joy of Brie's life, and the sadness gradually stepped back with time. Sometimes, when we're sitting on the porch and I look up at the stars, I think they're not stars at all but windows in heaven for Brie's spirit to shine through, letting us know she's all right. She never grew old. She'll stay six forever.

* * *

I run with my Mom in the mornings, just like we've always done, and in the afternoons after she comes home from school, we walk to the shops or go to the river. When my Dad has his time off from work, we all go to our beach together. Minh's started to take me running sometimes, which is one of those unexpected "best exceptions" you could ever ask for. He even bought a little black dawg named Quan for me to play with. His name means "warrior," but he's one of the smallest dawgs I've ever seen. I think a lot of little dawgs like to think they're big and strong. We chase each other around the garden and skim board across the tiles like Brie and I used to do, but it totally does him in because of his size, and before long, he trots back to his house and conks out for the rest of the day. When Minh goes to see his family on holidays, he puts Quan in the basket of his motorbike with his bird. They sit right next to each other, except the bird's in a paper bag. I know if it wasn't, it would fly away, but it still seems pretty weird.

I've gone to a lot of places with my Humans since Brie left. Sometimes, we go to Jessie's or someone else's house for lunch or dinner, and other times, we'll go on a completely new outing. If my Mom and Dad have errands to do, they always take me with them in the taxi and I wait in the car. We've found a new Vina van, with a driver who's not afraid of me and can understand my Mom and Dad's Vietnamese, so life's a little easier on that side. When my Mom and Dad go to do their chores or have lunch, Mr. Thanh and I sit in the van together, and he's happy to "singsong" with me until they come back. I'm also allowed to run on the field at my Mom's school if there's nothing's going on that involves a ball, and sometimes we eat lunch at the restaurant on the river, then run home.

They've even taken me to a fancy restaurant that's truly dawg-friendly, like the one ARCEA goes to in New York. It's called Binh An and has this beautiful stretch of green along the river and flower gardens everywhere. My Mom and Dad sit out near the water under a canopy and have a snack and a glass or three of something before lunch, and I can run on the grass as long as I don't stop and trim the flowers, which is always tempting. Before my Mom and Dad eat, it's back and forth, back and forth, between the lawn and the river, where they're in ree-lax mode for a quite a long time. We always bring a tennis ball so they can wear me out before we go to our table.

Sometimes, Danielle, the French owner, has her dawgs there, too, or I hang around with other dawgs who have come for lunch like me. Danielle is a true dog lover, which is the best kind of Human there is, as far as I'm concerned. When she says "Har-eee," it's with the same soft roll of her tongue as Phuong and Louisa, which makes my knees weak and my heart jump. She doesn't mind if her guests bring their dawgs either, and she's always telling us we're there to ree-lax and enjoy the day, just like our Humans.

One of the best things about Binh An is a jazz band that plays through lunch and into the afternoon. I lie there quietly listening to Danielle sing and watching all the Humans dancing. The feeling is pure happiness. When they play "It's a Wonderful World," every-one sings, because it's a special song for Vietnam that all the expat Humans know and love. Sometimes, we while away the whole after-noon, and when we finally leave, the sun is setting in all different shades of crimson and gold.

We always go to Binh An in a taxi, but a few times, we've come back by boat, and I can't begin to tell you what an amazing feeling it is to be zooming down the Sông Sài Gòn in a speedboat. At first,

it reminded me of driving around in Lemon Loaf with the breeze brushing against my muzzle, but once we got going, it was way more exciting—not to fault Lemon Loaf or anything. It's just different. First of all, you're on the water, and second, you go about twenty hundred times faster. It's as awesome as anything you've ever done in your life!

The river's always flat calm and the boat flies along like a dream over glass, going so fast we're almost airborne. The colors of the sky are painted on the water, and when I look behind me, there are waves rolling out to all the beaches along the river.

Once, I got to sit right up front beside the captain, who drove with one hand on the wheel and the other on my shoulder, like we were a real team. The only thought I had as we were speeding along with the wind on my back and the sun shining warm on my face was "Puh-leeze don't let this ever end!"

We zing past our beach then tie up at a pier in the BP compound for expats, and sometimes we stop in and see Jessie on the way home. Once or twice, she's even been at Binh An when we've been there, and we've hung out together and come home on the same boat.

* * *

Of all my unforgettable memories since the first day I met my Humans, there are a few that stand out far above the others. The most vivid, of course, are of Brie: the day we brought her home to a place where she knew she'd be safe, the day she went on ahead of us and every joyful moment in between. She changed our lives forever.

But something new has come into our house recently that's affecting us in the same Golden, heart-warming way. She has a name; in fact, she has quite a few names considering she just got here, but for now, I'm going to introduce her as Mali. Like Brie's story, Mali's has to be told all on its own, though I'm worried you won't believe this one incredible part. Even my Humans, who spent hours and hours researching on the computer, were astounded when they finally confirmed a remarkable connection. But they checked and rechecked and were able to prove without a shadow of a doubt that Mali's story is true. I don't want to give it away, but actually it's *our* story.

CHAPTER 11
When Harry Met Mali

I always know when my Humans are going away. The telltale signal, like the kennel in the kitchen, is the suitcase in the bedroom just before they leave. Depending on the size, I can usually get an idea of whether it's going to be a short or a never-ending wait at the gate until they come back. There's one particularly long time away they call "Home Leave." Home Leave, my paw! It's more like "leave home" forever, because when it happens, you swear they're never coming back.

The suitcase, or suitcases, usually comes out of "the store" a few sleeps before their actual departure. "The store" is this closet where they keep all their travel bags, our Science Diet and other items they don't want us getting into. Once it's made its way into the bedroom, the bag sits in a corner for a while, looking completely non-threatening, but trust me, it doesn't stay that way for long. As soon as they start filling it up with these nice, neat little piles that smell like them, it loses every bit of its innocence. I'd even go so far as to say it becomes tainted. After the first pile's gone in, I start sliding into a funk, knowing they're leaving and I'm not. Within minutes, I'm at rock bottom, sprawled out lifelessly on the floor with my head completely inside the bag, resting on a pile of my Mom's bras or my Dad's underwear. I mean, how pathetic is that?

Normally, when they're going out, I thunder down the stairs beside them and let them rub my ears and say their good-byes without any separation anxiety whatsoever, but if there's a suitcase in the equation, it's a totally different scenario, simply because I know they're going to close it, carry it downstairs, walk out to a taxi and drive away. There's not even a remote chance they'll be home for dinner that night, the next or the next!

Of course, I have to take my head out when it's time to close it, but that's as far as I go to accommodate them. After that, I bury it between my paws and stay there, flopped out like a rag doll, looking more pitiful than before. A lot of Humans think we do this deliberately to make them feel guilty, but they're wrong. We can't pretend everything's okay when it's not, and if the situation were reversed they'd do exactly the same thing

For all I know, the suitcase may have already made its way to the front porch and out to the gate with Minh, but I'm so despondent at this point, I wouldn't have a clue if it had. But they haven't gone anywhere, at least not yet. They're still in the bedroom, crouched down beside me with their heads buried in my fur, whispering, "We're going to miss you so much, Har, but we absolutely promise we'll be back very, very soon." And…therein lies the rub—they're glossing over the truth again to make me feel better. Their intentions may be good, but "very, very soon"? I don't think so! Even if it isn't a lie, soon is never soon enough, which is why I simply can't go downstairs when suitcases are involved and stand there, watching them drive off into the sunset.

The worst times are when the giant overseas bags come out and they leave for much longer periods, with me waiting endlessly at the gate, lying there wistfully, listening for some signal—the smallest sign—that they're coming back. Thankfully, my Mom usually goes ahead of my Dad and he comes back first, so it's not quite as torturous as it would be if they were both gone for the entire time.

Anyway, one of their "roller derbies" appeared in the upstairs hall the other day and made its way to their bedroom. That's what they call their little suitcases with wheels (?!!?), which are not generally cause for a major slump, simply because they're too small to cross the pond and stay for a long time. Thank Dawg—this wasn't going to be an extended holiday. The other giveaway was there were so few piles inside I couldn't get comfortable, but I hung in there anyway to make my point.

Just before dinner, we went to Jessie's house and came home with a small pink kennel. My Mom put a tag on it and set it by the door. "VeLLy interesting," I thought. The kennel was going wherever she was. The next day, Mr. Thanh, my new very best taxi driver friend, came in the middle of my morning nap to pick her up, and she left— but not before ruffling my fur and whispering in my ear, "Just you wait, Hars. I have a wonderful surprise for you!"

It had been two dinners and one restless night without her, plus a futile wait at the gate for my Dad the second night. I'd actually given up and gone into the kitchen to see if there was anything cooking when I heard Mr. Thanh's horn. By the time I got outside, his van was parked in the driveway and my Mom was getting out with something in her arms. In the next breath, they were both beside me, my Dad scratching behind my ears like he does and my Mom bending down to give me a glimpse of what she was holding against her chest.

It looked like one of my fluffy toys, except it was moving; in fact,

its little body was quivering from head to toe. My Mom stooped down so that I could get a better look. Two big brown eyes gazed up at me, and I knew immediately. It was a puppy. Not a long-legged one like Brie when she first came home—much smaller—but a puppy all the same. And it wasn't just any puppy. It was a Golden like me, with huge oversized paws. "Harry," my Mom said, beaming at me. "I want you to meet your new little sister, Mali."

She already had a name when she was born, but my Mom had changed it in Chiangmai, where she'd gone to get her. Mali (meaning "jasmine" in Thai) is the name of the delicate little white flowers in our garden that make us all goofy with their beautiful, intoxicating scent. I decided right then and there that she'd grow up to be just like them: a little goofy and beautiful at the same time. She already was beautiful; in fact, she looked like a little angel.

My Mom put her down on the grass and she sat there perfectly still with her tiny pink tongue peeking out one side of her mouth. She looked too scared to move, but after a while, she stood up, squatted and peed, then sat down again with her head cocked to one side and her eyes cast downward.

We were spellbound, watching every move she made, even if it was just the pulses of her breathing. My Mom and Dad both had those glassy, glazed expressions they get on their faces when they're totally euphoric about something. Every once in a while, my Mom would

scratch behind my ears and tell me not to worry, I'd always be her "beauty boy," then we'd watch Mali some more. For some reason, I wasn't worried.

When she lay down, she splayed her legs way out to the side, and even after she stopped being a "puppy puppy," she lay in the same position. For a while they called her their "yoga dawg," but when she started standing on two legs on the stool in the kitchen to reach the counter, they changed her nickname to "Circus Dawg."

For the first few days, she was mostly in the kitchen or out on the lawn, lying with her nose buried between her paws or sitting with her head bowed demurely. Every time I went near her, her fluffy little body would tremble all over and she'd look at me with the fear of Dawg in her dark, watery eyes. But little by little, she became less timid, licking my Mom and Dad's faces affectionately and enticing me to play by planting herself in front of me like Brie used to do.

She sleeps in her kennel beside their bed at night with some of her new toys plus some of mine, and during the day it's moved to the kitchen. She goes inside whenever she's tired, which is about 90 percent of the time. I swear, she spends most of her life in there. There were newspapers all over the kitchen floor when she first arrived, but they haven't been there since she started tearing them to bits—not just shredding them but chewing the entire paper, including the sports section—and then swallowing every last piece. My Dad takes it all in stride, which I find a bit weird considering his obsession with sports, but I think when you're a puppy you basically get away with murder. Now she's chewing whatever she can get her razor-edged little teeth into: paper, books, magazines, the carpet, the corners of the table, shoes, socks, metal, plastic—she doesn't care.

When my Mom came home from Chiangmai, she brought all these papers about Mali, except she wasn't called Mali at first, she was called Area's Little Goldrush Sarah Lee—go figure (?!!?). Anyway, they've been spending night after night huddled over the computer, looking for something. They even found a picture of my real Dad. I can't say I've ever given any thought to having another Dad besides my Human one, but I guess I do. He's a lot bigger than I am, and his name is Goldsmith Captivator, which sounds like a gladiator. My Mom looked up the meaning of my name in a book the other day, and it said it meant "home ruler," which must be what I am.

So now it's like day 4 or 93 or whatever, and they're still poring over those papers until they're bleary-eyed, mumbling things like "Calinours Promises Promises, Goldwing Rhythm 'n' Blue and Gold Rush Charlie." Hullo!?

WHOA! There appears to have been a breakthrough! They're completely beside themselves, flying around the house in a manic state, shouting at the top of their lungs: "We've figured it out. We've got it!" It's incredible!" Whatever *it* happens to be!

Now, even though I don't understand the words, my instinct is telling me this is huge. So I'm going to repeat what I just heard, word for word, because *you*, the reader, being Human, will understand what they mean and the magnitude of their discovery. Trust me, it *is* incredible!

"Honey (that's what my Dad calls my Mom sometimes), this is unbelievable! Harry's grandfather, Goldwing True Bear, is Mali's great-great-great-grandfather! Tell me, what are the chances of that happening? About one in a million? It's astonishing!

My Mom: "We've made ALL the connections?"

My Dad: "Yup! Every single one of them. Come and look; it's right here!"

My Mom: "My Gawd! No one is going to believe this! No one!"

It's not just a coincidence. It's a miracle. Yours truly, Harry Cleveland Brown Howard, formerly Calinours Harry Cleveland Brown, from Vancouver, British Columbia, Canada, and Mali, my new little sister, formerly Area's Little Goldrush Sarah Lee, from Chiangmai, Chiangmai Province, Thailand, are from the same family, even though we were born 7,112 miles apart. It's beyond amazing!

You've already seen a picture of me with my Dad when I was a puppy—basically a little fluff ball like Mali and a little bit *"pum pui,"* as Tui, my VBF in Thailand, used to say. Well, here's another photo of me beside one of Mali when she first started going out for walks.

Same same, right? And even though mine's not a front view, you can totally tell we're related.

She doesn't really like being on a lead, but she's going a little farther every day, so I think she's getting used to it. She's also started running after our Dunlops and bringing them back, then shredding them like I do. It's like every single thing we do is the same.

Her next phase, after chewing everything in sight, has been getting into everything out of sight: drawers and cupboards, laundry baskets, visitors' suitcases and Minh's part of the house when he forgets to pull the gate across or shut the side door to the spare room where Viet Ha and Vien Ha from my Dad's office in Hanoi stay when they come to work in Ho Chi Minh City. When they're not there, I go into their room to get away from it all, and when they're there, I go in to just *be* with them.

Get this. The other day I'd wandered into their room for some peace and quiet. There are three beds side by side, just in case someone extra comes from Hanoi, and I was standing between two of them pondering what to do next—you know how you do—when Mali comes in, leaps up onto a bed and proceeds to walk across my back to get to the next one as if I was the Sài Gòn Bridge. I couldn't believe it, and after her first crossing, she had the gall to walk back. My Mom saw the whole thing, and when she phoned my Dad to tell him, she was laughing so hard she could hardly speak.

* * *

Nothing is sacred anymore—in the house, the garden or outside the gate. I thought I was bad with Off Limits and roadside cuisine, but compared to Mali, I'm a model of good behavior. She's a regular little garbage disposal, yet our Mom and Dad are still coming up with endearing names for her in their gushing tones. This week, she's "Our Little Angel." She does a very good imitation, with her innocent chocolate-brown eyes, though when you look closely, you can see they're glowing with mischief. The name couldn't be more deceptive.

She ate her first offering this week. A Thai man had put it out for a special Buddha day, and my Mom had to take flowers to him yesterday and apologize about a hundred times. "*Koh tok, koh tok, koh tok, koh tok*" (sorry, sorry, sorry, sorry). It was so embarrassing.

If you've never been to Asia, you probably don't know about offerings, but for us, they're sort of like a rite of passage, so I think I should describe them and explain their significance. Brie and I first came across offerings in Thailand. They were everywhere. There aren't as many in Vietnam, because they're put inside temples not at the side of the road, but every once in a while we run into them because there are Thai people in our neighborhood. The first time you see one from a distance, you can easily mistake it for regular roadside cuisine, but when you get closer, it's like WHOA! This is on such a completely different level; it's an insult to talk about roadside and offerings in the same breath. Why? Because offerings are sacred.

If you don't know what sacred means, it's something that's kind of Gawdlike and untouchable in a pure, awesome sort of way, and you're supposed to just leave it alone; in fact, you should probably bow your head when you walk past. I'm not really sure you absolutely have to do this, but it just seems like a nice, respectful thing to do, seeing as Humans put offerings out to remember something or someone in their family. Having said this, I'm the first to admit they're almost impossible to resist and it takes all the restraint you can muster to ignore them. But it helps "if you can keep your head when all about you are losing theirs"[10] (i.e., Mali) and remind yourself your bad behavior will humiliate your Mom, possibly even banish her from the neighborhood,

---

10   "If" by Rudyard Kipling. The initial publication of the poem was in the "Brother Square Toes" chapter of *Rewards and Fairies*, a collection of Kipling's poetry and short fiction published in London by Macmillan and Co., Ltd., 1910, Octavo.

cost her money for flowers and you a severe reprimand. Still, all you can do is your best.

Once you've seen one, you'll be able to spot them for the rest of your life, because of the way they're displayed and the extraordinary blend of scents that wafts up from them. Whereas your day-to-day roadside is just kind of plunked down on the road, offerings are placed deliberately on a corner or in front of a shop house. And talk about the art of presentation—you can't believe it. There's this unbelievable attention to detail. I mean it's light-years away from the usual pile of splintered chicken bones or half-eaten cobs of corn.

Just feast your eyes on this array of dishes that was on a street corner near our house recently, arranged perfectly on a plastic plate like a mini TV dinner: jasmine rice with a glob of shrimp paste on top; chicken with hot chilies; *nước mắm*, the rancid fish sauce that I love and you can smell from across the river; and water in a yogurt container with plastic wrapping to keep the ants away. To finish it off, there were three little red-and-gray joss sticks placed delicately over the rice, their exotic scent drifting our way. It was truly something to behold!

Mali didn't have a clue what an offering was until the other day when we were out on our 4 p.m. walk, but boy, she sure does now! We were on a laneway off the river road when she spotted it. I missed the actual grab, and it wasn't until I felt my Mom's tug on the other leash and heard her holler that I realized there was a full-on situation in progress. When I turned around, Mali was madly chomping down the entire contents of the tray: the rice, the chicken, the sauce, the cookies, the water, the wrapping and the joss sticks, which thank Dawg, weren't lit. Three chomps and that was it—everything was gone, well before my Mom jogged the choke collar a second time, crouched down to her level and shouted in the harshest training voice she's used so far, "No…Mali, No!" Too late. I could see Mali didn't have the slightest idea what she'd done, because right after she'd been reprimanded, she sat down beside the empty tray, gazed intently up at my Mom with her irreproachable eyes and proceeded to lick my Mom's face from top to bottom.

It's a nightmare these days. She runs around the house from morning till night, charging up the stairs, taking two at a time effortlessly and combing every room in search of anything she can find to chew on. As soon as she hears the sound of a cupboard opening in the kitchen, she comes thundering down, stopping for a snack if there is one and a drink from the toilet bowl, before heading outside to start digging her zigzaggy trenches in the garden. Every day there's major collateral damage, but nothing compares to her most recent caper. It was her speed and agility, her habit of getting into anything and everything and her obsession with chewing and swallowing paper that gave her the wherewithal to pull off a real honest-to-Dawg heist. She's gone far beyond newspapers and magazines. She's discovered money, and it's turned her into a common thief.

* * *

A Situation in Saigon: Mali's Heist

(Recounted by Harry in the style of Sergeant Joe Friday from the 1950s radio and TV detective series *Dragnet*. Friday was well known for his clipped, deadpan delivery, influenced by the hard-boiled school of crime fiction of the day.)

Dum-du-dum-dum…dum-du-dum-dum…dah.

The story I am about to tell is true. The names have NOT been changed to protect anyone.

This is the city—Ho Chi Minh, formerly Saigon, Vietnam. From one day to the next, it's never the same. They make it that way. Including the suburbs, millions live here: people, dawgs, cats, Brahma bulls, water buffalo, you name 'em. Some have something to give, but others are here to take away. It can be for pleasure, or simply because it's here to take. You never really know.

It was Friday, August 22, 2003—hotter than Hades in Saigon. My partner and I were about to start our afternoon rounds with our Mom. My partner's, Mali, a Golden Retriever puppy. She eats paper. Her boss is my Mom, dawg lover and full-time cop, a sergeant to boot. She works the day and night division wherever we happen to be. It can be tough having a cop around 24/7, especially when she's your Mom. Good friends like Jessie, stop by for a visit and a lady with a badge answers the door. The air turns frosty and the temperature drops a good 30 degrees. My name's Harry. I'm an expat Retriever and pretty grown-up.

4:30 p.m. the same day:

The Brahma bull had just sauntered past on his way to the pool hall, and I was in the garden waiting for my partner, Mali, and my Mom. We were about go out on our own saunter when our Mom realized she'd forgotten her watch. She ran upstairs to get it. As she entered the bedroom, she saw her purse lying on the floor. The contents were strewn everywhere: lipsticks, blush-on, mosquito repellent, a hair dryer, a coffee cup, a pair of shoes, a small photo album, a screwdriver, a ruler—the usual paraphernalia found in a woman's purse, except…something was missing. Her wallet—the brown one she keeps her money in.

4:32 p.m.:

She followed the paper trail down the stairs and out onto the porch. It ended there. Mali was nowhere to be seen. She walked around to the far side of the house and came in the other door, then did two more rounds. No sign of a suspect. *A* suspect?? *The* suspect.

She called to Minh, who was on the opposite side of the garden. Had he seen Mali? He started to babble.

"Stop babbling, Minh. Just the facts."

No, he hadn't.

4:39 p.m.: The Crime Scene

They both ran toward Minh's place, entering through the open

accordion door. They spotted her immediately. She was lying on one of the beds, clutching the wallet desperately between her paws, working her mouth as hard as she could to finish off the job. The few remaining bits were all that was left of twelve brand-new, crisp fifty-thousand dong notes and five ten-thousands. She'd had the rest for dinner. One side of the wallet was completely empty. She had good taste; she hadn't touched the worthless dirty dong on the other side. A huge grin spread across her face as they approached.

Saturday, August 23:

It all came out in the wash as she went about her business on the lawn the next day. There was enough evidence to put her away for good: corners of fifty dong notes and tattered fragments of Uncle Ho's face! They only needed one more thing—her statement. They never got it.

Saturday, September 13:

They assumed that was the end of it. Big mistake. Never assume. Not long after Mali's first heist, a good friend from our Mom's school came for dinner. They forgot to warn her. She left her purse on the floor in the kitchen. Bad idea. When she went to get it later, most of her money was gone. She collected a few pitiful bits and put them together in a thank-you note she sent a week later. Uncle Ho was clearly visible. The case was open and shut. It was the smell of the dong that did it. Her preference is big notes, but she'll take whatever she can get.

She acquired a new name after her second caper. It's used a lot, especially around our house, and is in bold letters above her mug shot on the fridge. She's known as Malice of An Phú. There's nothing new about being a common thief. Jails in Vietnam are full of them. They have only one thing on their mind: to steal.

"When you live in a society, you either live by the rules or by democratic process, you change 'em. You don't break them."

CHAPTER 12
Closing In on Ho Chi Minh City

My Mom said something to me the other day that really got me thinking. We'd gone where we often go in the late afternoon, to a no-name beach in the opposite direction from Coconut Landing and were sitting by the river, watching Mali digging; birds swooping and rising; the palms bending with the breeze; a lizard skittering past, barely visible against the tall grass; and streaks of sunlight distancing themselves in the sky. It was as though it dawned on her for the very first time. "Do you know, Hars," she exclaimed "you're getting a little white around your muzzle." Then she rubbed my nose and scratched under my chin.

"Mmmh," I thought to myself. She's telling me my fur's changing from Golden to white. My Dad has had a white muzzle and white hair for quite a long time, and my Mom's hair seems whiter every time she turns around. One of the children from her school even said, "Teacher JuRie, I thought everyone who had white hair was dead," so it must happen at a pretty old age.

Next thought: If I'm getting a white muzzle, too, I'm probably about the same age as my Humans, but I don't have the foggiest idea how old that is. And even if I did, it wouldn't mean anything to me,

because I don't understand age and numbers. But you know how it is when you get your head around something. You have to stay with it.

I'd been to Hong Kong and back by the time we got Brie, so I was much older than she was, and I'm light-years ahead of Mali, who should be coming out of puppyhood any day but isn't close. The way things are going, she could stay there forever, and whether she grows up or not, she's going to have to live with the humiliation of being labeled a common thief. I have noticed there's a tendency for my Dad and his friends to lose their hair at this particular stage of their lives. I don't know where it goes, but it doesn't really matter, because once it's gone, it's gone. Fortunately, I don't think we have to worry about it.

Since we came back from our swim yesterday morning, my Mom's been cooking, cooking, cooking non-stop, even last night after my Dad and Mali and I had gone to bed. And when we came down this morning, the table in the dining room was set for something festive, with beautiful flowers and lots of places for people to sit and eat. There are balloons everywhere and all these pictures of my Dad (pre–white hair and muzzle) on the tables beside my sofa.

It was the smells drifting out of the kitchen that made us cut our normal 7:25 to 8:00 a.m. time slot in the garden short so that we could head back for breakfast ASAP and check out Action Central. We managed to squeeze everything into less than half the time it usually takes by attending to our "business" right away instead of futzing around forever trying to find the perfect spot, doing our speed laps in one huge record-breaking blur, not going anywhere near the little white flowers that grind us to a hazy halt and acknowledging the new lowlife with a bark instead of our usual badgering.

The kitchen was buzzing. There were pots and pans and dishes everywhere, some bubbling over the stove, others going in and out of the oven and more on the breakfast table covered with the plastic wrap Mali has added to her eating repertoire recently. There was also a cake that wasn't there last night on the top shelf of the corner cupboard. Between all the chopping, cutting and stirring my Mom and Minh were doing, they were flying back and forth across the kitchen to grab things out of the fridge.

As soon as we came into the kitchen with my Dad, I heard my Mom call out in this singsongy voice she uses when she wants to be Irish: "Aye…Good Mornin' to yu, Mickey! Eight…eight…forty-four…wuz it ten? Quite sum time ago, to be shere! But you're comin' along rather nicely, don't yu tink? My Gawd, I mean fere sixty yeers, yer not doin' too budly a-tall. May good luck pursue yu mornin', noon and night, und may yu live to be a hundred with wun extra year to rupent. Huppy Berrthday!"

And that's when I knew. My Dad was sixty, and maybe I was, too. A few minutes later, everyone was back at work and the kitchen was humming again. I planted myself right next to the fridge, where Minh and my Mom couldn't miss me gazing up at them every time they turned around. And guess who sashayed over and sat down right next to me? No matter where I go these days, she's right behind me, which I guess is a little sister thing. She also copies me a lot. I mean, check out the body language. Not only has she perfected her own gaze, she's figured out that as soon as she looks at a Human with her watery chocolate-brown eyes, she reduces them to a state where they are totally incapable of saying NO to anything.

We sat there almost perfectly still for three of our regular time slots, but the time flew by and it turned out to be one of the high points of our week. First of all, we'd shown how quick we can be with our routine if there's something pressing, and second, we'd been generously rewarded for our patience. I actually thought Mali's little tummy had

simply had enough when she bolted, but it was just her radar kicking in and telling her she needed a run, and so did I. We'd missed our speed laps before we went on duty in the kitchen and had all this pent-up energy inside.

When we need a really good work-out, we don't do our regular speed laps; we do our fartlek running, which is not what you think it is but the absolute best thing in the world for building up stamina. If you're not very athletic, you've probably never heard of it, but it can turn you into an all-round athlete in no time at all if you put your mind to it. I mean, that's how powerful it is. It means "speed play" in some other language, but I'm not sure which one. I don't think it's Vietnamese.

A lot of Humans do it when they're getting ready to run a really long race, like a marathon, but anyone can do it. You just start running these incredibly fast sprints the width of your garden and back, going faster and faster, until all anyone can see is this mad, whirling fuzzball, and you don't stop until you're hyperventilating and your entire body is on the verge of collapse.

We usually slide into a coma right afterward, except on that day, one of those annoying signals suddenly went off in our brains and we had to abort the nap plan at the sound of the bell. It was the old Pavlov association response coming at us totally out of the blue.

In case you don't recognize the name, Mr. Ivan Pavlov was this very famous dawg scientist who won a huge prize for noticing that right after 90 percent of dawgs (the other 10 percent being either tone deaf or not the cleverest canines in the kennel) hear a bell, we make an immediate connection and do whatever we're supposed to do. It's like catching a whiff of something putrid and having that power inside take hold and switch you over to automatic pilot, except Mr. Ivan Pavlov didn't explain it that way. He said it was "a conditioned response," which was scientific enough

for him to win this amazing prize called the No-Bell, which is totally weird because there's always a bell—it's the whole basis of his theory. Hullo, whoever gave Mr. Pavlov's prize its name!

Anyway, the second we hear our door bell, we're on the move, and we were right behind our Dad when it rang. As soon as the gate opened, someone handed him a huge box, then we all walked back into Action Central, where he set it down on the counter in the middle of our kitchen. My Mom came over and oohed and awed about how beautiful it was, then read the writing on the top out loud: "Happy sixtieth, Michael."

The object of all the gushing was this absolutely enormous cake from Kinh Do Bakery, which makes the biggest, best cakes in all of Vietnam. I'd only seen a Kinh Do cake once before, when my Dad got one for my Mom's birthday. Whoops! BOINK! Another light just went on. My Mom's birthday can't possibly be the same day as mine and my Dad's, seeing as she's already had her Kinh Do cake, but it wasn't that long ago. Her cake had enough icing to fill our kitchen sink.

Anyway, they opened the box, even though you could see the cake through the cellophane, and found a card that said "Minh and Alex," who are two of my Mom and Dad's VBFs in Ho Chi Minh City. The cake was white with pink and yellow flowers all over it and chocolate writing on the top, and it was beautiful! Circus Dawg had to stand on her hind legs on her stool to get a look at it. I was beside her on two legs—no stool.

More oohing and awing, before they closed the box and my Dad put it on the counter by the phone.

My Mom: "No, not there! Bad idea."

My Dad: "Where then?"

My Mom: "In the girls' room on the desk. Make sure both doors are closed."

So the Kinh Do cake went into Viet Ha and Vinh Ha's room behind closed doors, and my Dad wandered upstairs to get his CDs ready. The activity in the kitchen was becoming more frantic by the second, with my Mom bringing out greens from the fridge, chopping a few, then leaving them on the counter before she was done so she could check the pots on the stove and the big dishes in the oven. My Dad had his CDs blasting, and the whole house was coming alive with music and excitement. Even though Mali didn't have a clue what was happening, she was doing her fly-pasts through the dining room, out the door, along the lap pool and back into the kitchen.

Everything seemed to be coming together, though my Mom and Minh were still running between the kitchen and the dining room, putting big baskets of flowers by the front door and candles on the table. I opted for a little snooze so that I'd be in prime form when the guests arrived and moseyed out to my favorite spot under the mango tree in the far corner of the garden. The well I'd made the day before was still there, and I settled into it easily, took a nice deep breath and let it go with a long sigh. The sun was streaming through the trees onto a patch of grass beside me, but it was cool and shady where I was and far enough from the house to be undisturbed. The only sounds were the occasional quiver of a leaf or the delicate flutter of wings above me.

I'd almost drifted off when I was startled by an incredibly shrill cry from inside—so shrill, in fact, that it made its way through the garden, over the wall and up the main street of An Phú. It wasn't a plaintive cry like my Mom's "Why, Harry, why?" when all I've done is borrowed a baguette, nor was it a painful yelp like Brie's in Hanoi. It was a cry of complete and utter shock and disbelief. And it didn't come from my Mom; it came from my Dad. Nor did it have my name attached to it; it had Mali's.

When I got there, they were standing with Minh by the open door to the girls' room with their mouths gaped open. There was a stunned sliver of silence, followed by loud, startled voices.

"How in Gawd's name did she do it?" from my Dad. "The door was closed!"

"I know!" from my Mom. "I saw it."

The door had not defeated her. Nothing had. She was standing on her hind legs on the chair, grinning from ear to ear, looking as though she'd just won the No-Bell Prize itself. Her entire face, neck and chest were covered in gobs of icing, and traces of cake and bits of cellophane were stuck to her fur. The cardboard box was in torn, tattered pieces on the floor with crumbs scattered around it, and the silver plate the cake had come on was licked clean. A long, multicolored streak of icing ran across the top of the desk, as though she'd deliberately left her mark. "I did it," it said. "I ate an entire Kinh Do cake for twenty-five Humans, just like that."

Two terrifying thoughts: The first wasn't what we could see *on* Mali but what we couldn't see *inside* her. The second was the ingredients for a white cake with butter icing of this size. The enormity of what she had in her stomach, as she stood there in her Circus Dawg stance, with her front paws resting on the desk and her head cocked to one side, looking at us with pure puppy dawg love was simply too overwhelming to grasp.

The estimated ingredients for the cake are:

Just under 5 pounds of butter
7 cups of white flour
22 egg whites
6 egg yolks
6 ½ cups of sugar
¾ cup of water
2 ½ cups of milk
8 tsp baking powder
2 Tbsp each of almond and vanilla extract
1 Tbsp of cream of tartar
5 squares of dark chocolate
Food coloring

My Dad said it was "inconceivable that any Human or canine could consume that amount in one fell swoop."

Unanswered and/or partially answered questions:

Did she push the door open, or did she actually turn the doorknob?

How did she do it without anyone hearing her? My Mom, Minh and my Dad were all in the general vicinity, though my Dad was upstairs and discovered her by pure chance when he came down and saw the open door.

How did she manage to chew and swallow the cake in the time it took me to go outside and settle in briefly for my nap, while my Mom and Minh were going between the dining room and the kitchen, passing right by Viet Ha and Vien Ha's room every time?

Answer: She didn't. She gulped it down in enormous, manic mouthfuls without bothering to chew.

Were Minh and my Mom so frazzled getting things ready that they tuned out everything around them?

All food for thought, so to speak.

Almost instantly, my Mom came out with: "Poor little thing. She sat in the kitchen so patiently with Harry all morning. Every time I looked at her, her sweet little face was so full of love and hope, and do you think any of us were paying the slightest bit of attention other than giving her the occasional baby tomato or tiny piece of chicken? No! I don't blame her. She was just bored."

They moved quickly. There was no reprimand. The clock was ticking, the deed was done and the cleanup had to get underway immediately. I heard "Let's go" and "Kinh Do" and saw my Dad and Minh running toward Minh's motorbike.

My Mom was over by the pool with Mali. She'd tied her to the fence with her long leash and was rigorously scrubbing and hosing her down. When she finished, she rubbed her affectionately with a fluffy white towel, gave her a big hug and left her there to dry. Mali didn't look sick, but after a few minutes, she lay down, splayed her legs out behind her, pushed her nose between her paws and conked out. Cold!

My Mom headed straight to the crime scene, removed the remains of the box from the floor and vacuumed up the few remaining remnants of the cake. When she was done, she went to the phone and called someone, but it was just the usual outpouring of Human mumbo jumbo—"Blah, blah, blah, Mali" (?!!?) "Blah, blah, blah, cake" and "Thank you." Then she roused Mali, put her on her short leash and took us both upstairs while she showered and changed.

Minh and my Dad were back in no time. My Dad rushed upstairs.

My Dad: "What did she say?"

My Mom: "Wait…watch. Lucky…not much chocolate. May be sick as a dawg or we may have to make her…"(?!!?).

My Dad: "And how exactly do we do that?"

My Mom: "Blah, blah, blah purrrr-ox-ide" (?!!?).

Go figure!

Another ring at the gate.

My Dad: "Well, we can count our blessings. The replacement's here."

To Minh: "I'd better check to make sure they got it right.

"Happy sixtieth, MikurL," he read out loud.

"MikurL! For Gawd's sake! They've written my name in Vietnamese English."

My Mom: "Who told them your name?"

My Dad: "Minh…"

My Mom: "Well…how would you expect him to spell it?"

So the cake traveled back to Kinh Do Bakery on the motorbike, and a little while later it showed up with my Dad's name in "English English." Alex and Minh were the first to arrive and heard the entire saga within minutes, dissolving into gales of laughter every time my Dad paused to catch his breath.

"Thank you…from Mali blah, blah, blah" (?!!?) "She loved… your Kinh Do…" By the time he got to "Minh…Moto and MikurL," they were laughing so hard, there were tears rolling down their faces.

Mali slept upstairs for most of the afternoon, and every so often, my Mom and I went up to check on her. When the sun had left the garden, she padded downstairs, looking terribly groggy and uncomfortable, ambled outside and grazed on grass and leaves. When she'd had enough, she came back in and flopped down on the floor near the sofa. Somehow, she managed to sleep, seemingly oblivious to the music, the laughter and everything that was going on around her, but when the birthday cake came out and everyone stood and sang to my Dad, I swear I saw the corners of her mouth turn up into a satisfied smile. A deep sigh and her face was back to an angelic look of sweet repose. I stayed near my Mom or Dad's feet, feeling their warmth and that kind of happiness that's impossible to describe.

* * *

Mali and I awoke the next morning to the cries of the neighbor's rooster. Long, languid stretches before we meandered over to opposite sides of the bed. Our first nudges were ignored and the second brought pitiful pats on our heads that told us our Mom and Dad weren't getting up anytime soon. We flew down the stairs.

The only signs of my Dad's special birthday were a few balloons on the floor in one corner of the dining room, the sweet smell of flowers and lingering aromas from the kitchen. We immediately raced out the back door into the garden. Dawn had given way to bright sunlight and squeaky-clean air. Even the trees seemed to be waking up, rustling their leaves as if they were shaking themselves off and stretching their limbs after a long snooze, just like we do.

In a heartbeat, we were zooming in and out of the flower beds, sniffing like regular old Bloodhounds, checking out new leaf litter, lowlife, mango pits, tennis balls, coconuts—any and every distraction we came across. Mali took timeouts to attend to more business than usual, but when we went to the beach later, she was back to her lively self again, tearing up and down the beach and moving like lightning through the water. My Mom said she was "on a sugar high, which was totally understandable," except when it was time to go, she was suddenly exhausted and they practically had to drag her home. A few bites of her Science Diet, a sloppy drink of water and she was padding up the stairs as if she were the oldest puppy in all of Vietnam. When we went up after dinner, she was curled up in a tight little ball at the end of the bed, sleeping like a baby. She'd had her first and last Kinh Do cake.

CHAPTER 13

Finishers and Finished in Ho Chi Minh City

Mali—AKA Malice, Yoga Dawg, Circus Dawg, Little Angel and Picture of Innocence—is growing up before our eyes. Her legs are still shorter than mine, but we can wrestle head to head on our hind legs now until one of us gets the upper paw. She wasn't born to run like Brie, but what she lacks in form, she makes up in sheer will and determination, and the look on her face the moment she's let off her lead and breaks into full flight, bounding toward the beach or across the field for her ball as fast as her little legs will carry her, is worth its "wait" in gold. She's won her way into our hearts and works the same magic with everyone she meets. I don't even mind it when she copies me or follows me anymore. She's Mali, and like her name, she's

beautiful and goofy at the same time. She's also my little sister and my VBF in the whole world.

It's rainy season, so we have to stay in way more than usual; otherwise, we could be mistaken for two enormous drowned rats or, even worse, be swept

185

away with the live ones we see floating down our street every day. One day it just starts coming down in buckets, and it doesn't stop for months. Halfway in from our gate to the door in that driving rain and you're soaked right through to the bone. It's like someone upstairs has turned on these gigantic taps and nothing can stop them.

Before a downpour, the air is noticeably hot and heavy, so you can usually sense when it's coming, but every once in a while, we get caught. It's almost always in the late afternoon, and we have to huddle together under a shop house awning and wait it out with everyone else. As soon as there's a break, we make a run for it, but you don't know wet until you go through *mùa mưa* in Vietnam.

If Minh picks up my Mom at school and the skies let loose before they get home, she has to drag her feet through the water the rest of the way. And if his bike stops, which it usually does, because *xe oms* aren't supposed to travel through streets turned to rivers, she has to get off and wade through "all that filthy sludge." She's not a happy camper when she walks in the door, I can tell you that, and she looks like a drowned rat, too, even though she always wears her purple rain cape.

My Dad thinks the *xe om* drivers "have ESP during *mùa mưa*," which is this extra sense that tells them when the skies are going to open up. Before the first drop hits the ground, every single moto driver in Ho Chi Minh City has donned his rain cape and is weaving colorful patterns through the streets, illuminating the city with red, orange, pink, green, yellow and purple streaks as they make their way through water up to their wheels, picking up and dropping off their passengers.

We can pretty much count on at least one huge downpour a day. In between, we just stick to our normal schedules, making adjustments

when we have to. The garden is lush with every shade of green, and we sometimes get tangled up in overgrown leaves and trailing vines when we go in and out of our trenches. At night, we can barely hear ourselves think with the constant croak of the frogs and the deafening drone of the cicadas that seem to love the rain as much as life itself.

My Mom says she "can actually see things growing" during rainy season, and that someone she knew actually watched some bamboo coming right up out of the ground, which sounds to me like another case of a Human not telling it like it is. I mean, I knew my paws were getting bigger, but I didn't actually see them growing in real time. But the garden sure glistens from all those showers and the scents are as fresh as the rain. Then, BINGO! Almost as quickly as it starts, it's over. Somebody turns off the taps and we're back to Hot and Hotter, with the fans whirling and humming upstairs and all the old customers lined up at the barber shop. Excuse me? What shop?

* * *

Our last days in Ho Chi Minh City must have come when *mùa mưa* had finished that year, because I remember being full of the joy of sunlit mornings and fun-filled days and the quiet that comes with moonlit nights. The rain had stopped, and it was Moon Festival. We even got to taste some moon cakes that were left out on the counter accidentally. Our Humans curse themselves whenever they do that, vowing "there won't be a next time," but there always is.

Almost overnight, there was an unsettling exception to our schedule. They seem to come like that—out of nowhere. You recognize there's been a change, but you don't know why, so it hangs over you, completely unraveling that part of your day. Other things keep going along like they always have, but you know it's just a matter of time before they change, too. I can't say there was only one exception; there were three disrupted time slots: our wake up/nudge time, our 8:00 to 8:30 a.m. and our 6:30 p.m. onward. And all of these had one common denominator: our Dad. They were our quality times with him, but he wasn't there anymore—not in the morning, most days or most nights.

It was almost the same as Chiangmai. He'd come home and stay when my Mom had a holiday from school. It would usually be after our dinner and she'd be futzing around in the kitchen when we'd hear the taxi pull up and the door open and close. We'd run to the gate, bursting with happiness, but two sleeps later he'd be gone again. Every time he left, he took another suitcase with him, and when he came home it would be empty. He'd fill it up and sometimes another and another until his closet was almost bare.

My Mom started doing a lot of work around the house: cleaning out cupboards, putting things in piles or boxes and giving a lot to Minh to take away. Then she went on a short trip with her roller derby, and Mali copied me and put her head on a pile of underwear inside it before she left.

Yup, you've got it. We're moving again; in fact, our Dad's already moved. When he comes back to see us, he's really just visiting. And the truck is going to be pulling up in front of our house any day and throwing us into total chaos.

On the bright side, we've been doing a fun family activity every time he comes home, which is going for very long runs together. We start out from the main road that goes to Coconut Landing, and instead of taking the turnoff like we usually do, we keep going past the big school and the BP compound filled with Human expats, past the An Phú supermarket and out along the straight road until we reach the narrow path and foot bridge that go to my Mom's school. And then we run all the way back. It was a bit hard for Mali at first, with her short little legs, but she's keeping up pretty well now. As soon as we get back, she crashes for the whole afternoon, which is okay because you have to make sure you have enough down time when you're running that far.

We've done the full run quite a few times without stopping, and when our Mom and Dad are ruffling our necks and giving us good strong massages afterward, they keep telling us we're ready, but we have no idea what we're ready for. Last night, they tried these sort of harnesses on us, except they were more like little blankets that went over our backs and tied under our bellies—one for Mali and one for me. They said they were "our bibs for the race," and they looked pretty awesome.

We got up super early today and drove to Saigon South in Mr. Thanh's taxi for our first ever Terry Fox Run (?!!?). Saigon South is this amazing place full of parks and green spaces, where you can walk and run for the whole day, if your Humans will let you stay that long. Our Mom and Dad always let us off our leads when we get to the far side, then use our Chuckit to throw our Dunlops to the Outer Limits.

When we got out of the car, Mr. Thanh smiled and said, "Good luck," and our Mom and Dad answered with "*Cám ơn,*" translated thank you in Vietnamese. We immediately joined streams of people wearing bibs just like ours—I'm talking zillions of Moms and Dads and children, all heading in the same direction. We stuck very close to our Mom and Dad while they blabbered away as if we understood every word they were saying, but there was one thing we couldn't possibly miss. It was the excitement in their voices and the running fever in the air. As more and more people joined the river of runners, the excitement just kept on building until we could hardly stand it. There was pure happiness everywhere we looked—shining down from the clear blue sky, glistening through the trees, beaming across people's faces, bouncing with every step and dancing to the beat of the music blaring out across Saigon South. And the most exciting thing of all was that Mali, yours truly and our Mom and Dad were part of it.

Almost all the Humans were carrying water bottles, and there were pretty girls selling T-shirts and hats all over the place. We didn't need T-shirts because we had our bibs, which our Mom and Dad had tied on before we left. I was 0001 and Mali was 0002, which were probably the luckiest numbers we could hope for! We also had our own hats that someone had brought us from a dawg shop in Canada, where they sell things like hats and cookies for dawgs to eat, not dawgs for people to eat.

After we'd stood around for a while, listening to the band and watching people jumping up and down to the music in "the staging zone," we went to a little fenced-in area with grass so that we could rest before we started. Lots of the kids from my Mom's school came in and sat with us while we waited. The Humans were all doing their warm-up stretches, some flat on their backs with one or both legs stretched way up in the air, aiming for the plough. Others doing Eastern yoga, like downward-facing dawg and even elbow stands. The only one doing the frog pose was Mali. I thought about doing a downward-facing dawg, but I was already stretched out on the grass with the kids massaging me, which was as good as anything.

As soon as our Mom and Dad came back, everyone started moving toward the start line, and when we got there, I felt the same exhilaration I always feel before a run, except it was a million times more, because the air was so charged. My Mom had my lead around her wrist and my Dad had Mali's, and we lined up with all the other runners, moving off to one side a little so that we wouldn't get trampled.

A man started speaking through a cone like Dr. Die's that made his voice almost unbearably loud. Mostly, he just rambled and every once in a while, there'd be a shrill screech from the cone and everyone would grit their teeth and cover their ears. We didn't understand a word he was saying, so it was hard for Mali and me to stay still. Besides, all we really wanted to do was get going. Everyone clapped and cheered when he finished, but I think it was just because he'd finally stopped talking.

Our Humans went into their standing stretches, where they balance on one leg like birds and pull the other one up behind them so that it touches their bums. It was our cue. I felt my Mom tighten her grip on my lead, and then she took my head in her hands like she does when she wants to lock her eyes into mine and tell me something super important, like "Guess where we're going, Har? For a car ride!" or "Har-eee, you know you're my beauty boy, don't you?" But she said neither, and what came out of her mouth next was the strangest thing I've ever heard from her.

The first part was fine and made perfect sense. "Okay, guys—it's time!" But the next part was totally inappropriate, and she even smiled when she said it. "Let's break a leg!" Excuse me? What on earth was she talking about? I had no choice but to shrug it off as one of those beyond perplexing things that comes out of your Human's mouth every so often. We had a race to run, and the man with the cone had just boomed out the first word Mali and I understood since he'd started his babble; in fact, we were so quick on the uptake that we reacted before the word had finished resonating through his cone. "GO!" We were off!

The pace was a little slow at first, with so many people, but they spread out quickly, and it wasn't long before we had our momentum and were running alongside our Mom and Dad perfectly in sync, like true runners. I swear, our hearts were so full we were almost flying. Whenever we heard "Go HaLLy, Go MaRi" from the children at my Mom's school and other Humans we knew, like Jessie's Mom and Dad, it gave us an extra spurt of energy and we'd pick up our pace and run even faster. Our Mom and Dad steered us over to water stations a few times so that we wouldn't get heat exhaustion, and the children poured water that we lapped up quickly so we wouldn't lose time.

I'm not sure how many laps we did around all the roads in Saigon South, but it was a lot, and trust me, crossing the finish line in your first big race is one of the most awesome feelings in the world. All these Humans who you don't even know are clapping and cheering and shouting like crazy, and suddenly you realize they're doing it for you. Even if you wanted to, you can't stop smiling, and after you're finished, you feel as though you can do anything you put your mind to.

Because you're a finisher, you get a special T-shirt with "Terry Fox Run" on the back and a certificate with your name on it that says "You Number One!" Then you get to drink a full bowl of Evian water and lie down on the grass in a nice shady spot, where you feel nothing but joy and fulfillment rushing through your body as people toddle over and massage your back. You don't really feel like rushing out and doing it all over again tomorrow, but you sure hope another time will come. That's Mali in her finisher's T-shirt. She was so exhausted she slept right through dinner.

* * *

It might have been the very next day that we went to see a nice new lady vet who had moved into the BP compound where Jessie lives. We had to get shots in our behinds, bright-blue tags on our leashes and some papers that said "Good Dawg, Harry" and "Good Dawg, Mali." My Mom gave the vet a picture of each of us and went back the next day to pick up these little books called passports.

The absolute coolest thing about having your own passport is that anyone who looks at it immediately knows you're an expat, frequent-flier, cross-culture canine. Here's mine (opposite page). Mali's is almost exactly the same, except it says Malice. Whoops! Sorry, sorry, I meant Mali. And it doesn't have her mug shot. It has a different picture, so no one will know her history as a felon. Actually, she's not a frequent flier like I am, because she's only been on a plane once, when we flew from Chiangmai to Ho Chi Minh City, whereas I've been on numerous jumbos.

Our Dad went away again and came home, went away again and came home, and then the truck arrived. Mali's antics were almost the

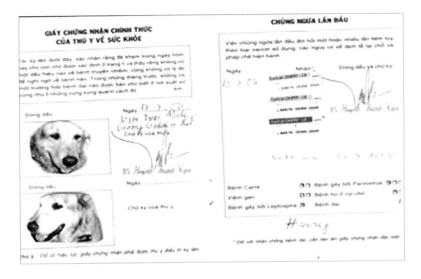

same as Brie's during her first pack-up, with the added dimension of
paper eating. She was in heaven with all that paper, especially the
bubble wrap she could pop in her mouth. Eventually, she had to be
tied up on her long leash.

One notable exception with this move was that the movers packed
our kennels, which are usually the only thing left behind for our
plane ride. A wishful thought. Maybe, just maybe, there was a new
PAW-LICY and we could loll around with our Mom and Dad in total
luxury on the upper deck, watching movies and eating boeuf bourgui-
gnon for dinner. But it didn't happen.

We stayed in an almost empty house for one more sleep, and the
next day a van like Hu`ng's arrived and parked in our driveway. My
Mom's big suitcases went in first, then a giant bag of our Science Diet
and a few smaller bags. Wherever we were going, we could get to by
car, which didn't really say much, seeing as if you wanted to you could
probably drive around the world for the rest of your life. After big
hugs from Minh and wags from us for Minh, Quan and the bird, Mali
and I got into the van. My Mom and Dad lingered on the front porch
with Minh, their good-byes and their sadness standing side by side.

CHAPTER 14
The Road to Cambodia

We settled in with my Mom and me in the seat behind the driver and my Dad and Mali behind us. Mostly we lay with our heads resting in our Mom and Dad's laps, but every so often, Mali would stand up and peer over the seat, look around, then flop back down. We must have gone a long way, because the sky was clear when we left An Phú, but when we woke up, it was *mùa mưa* all over again, with zigzaggy lightning shooting out from behind dark clouds and thunderclaps that made our hair stand on end.

I could see lights ahead, and moments later, we'd turned into a parking lot filled with buses and vans just like ours. By the time our leashes were on and our Mom and Dad had gathered up the small bags and hustled us out of the car, the rain was pelting down. The driver went on ahead with our suitcases and Science Diet, and we ran toward a building at the far end of the parking lot. Inside, we joined a long queue of sopping-wet Humans, with somber expressions on their faces, all standing waiting for something.

When our turn finally came, we found ourselves looking into the wide eyes of a tall, thin man at the counter in a green suit with a red star on his cap who appeared to be frozen on the spot. This prompted an "AHEM" from my Dad, which is a throat-clearing technique he uses in the mornings or when he wants to get someone's attention. We use a slightly more pleasant version when we need to remind the hand that feeds us that it's 6:02 and our dinner should be served at 6:00. After recovering from his initial shock, the man took our papers and disappeared behind the counter. When he popped up and handed them back to my Dad a few minutes later, he made a genuine attempt to smile. It must have been our size that undid him, plus he probably hadn't seen many dawgs with passports. We were out the door in a flash, making a mad dash on foot for "the border"—a tight little family of four, uncertain as to what lay ahead.

The wind-driven rain bounced off the pavement, stinging our faces and beating down hard on our backs. Mali and my Dad were in front, moving at a pretty good clip, and when my Mom and I finally managed to catch up, she had to shout to be heard. "It's not *Not Without My Daughter*,"[11] she called out (?!!?). "It's Not Without My Dawgs!"

We'd reached a wide-open, barren stretch of road when my Dad called back, "We're crossing no man's land. It's not theirs," pointing behind him, "and it's not theirs," pointing ahead" (?!!!?). It had to be someone's?

We kept on going until we came to a building with a red-and-blue flag flapping above it. Once we were inside, Mali and I shook ourselves off as maniacally as we possibly could, whipping our heads from side to side, wiggling our behinds, splattering water everywhere and making loud, spluttering *eum, eum, eum* sounds that are part of the ritual. All the Humans in the queue gave us nasty looks, which I didn't really understand, seeing as they could have done exactly the same thing and we wouldn't have cared less, but in no time, we were at the front of the line, and they were long gone.

This time we were looking into the sparkling eyes of a man in blue. After he lifted himself up off his stool to get a better look at us, his

---

11 A film with Sally Field crossing the Iranian border into Turkey with her young daughter in driving wind and rain.

mouth broke into a wide grin that lit up his whole face. Kindness radiated from his dark eyes, and I barked a *"xin chào"* to let him know he was already a NVBF. Mali copied me and he laughed out loud. He gestured to our Mom and Dad to step up to the counter, and after he'd looked at their papers and done something on his computer, he pointed to a camera. They smiled until it blinked, a few more stamps and they were done. "Welcome to Cambodia," he said with the same friendly smile. I was pretty sure I'd heard the name of our new country for the very first time.

We were next. He glanced at our pictures, then back at us, trying to figure out who was who. I don't think he really cared, because we're pretty much clones of each other, except for Mali's short little legs, but it was probably part of his job. He didn't make us gaze into the camera, so we gazed at him, and after he stamped our passports, we gazed at him some more. We kept on gazing until we were out the door. A nod, a smile and something that sounded like *"aw koon nah,"* but since we didn't know any of the language yet, it didn't mean anything to us. BOINK! A sudden revelation. Maybe this wasn't a singing language, which would have an amazingly positive effect on our Dad's life! No more shouting "An Phú" at 129 decibels or countless attempts to find taxi drivers who are willing to take him.

"Welcome to Cambodia, you three!" he chimed as we walked out the door, and that was that. We'd crossed another of those invisible lines our Humans understand far better than we do into a new country called Cambodia. I did have a fairly profound thought as I pranced along beside Mali and my Mom and Dad: There was no going back. We'd left our van in Vietnam.

No sooner had I got my mind around this major oversight, when a man standing near us pointed to an altogether different van. He must have read my mind.

"Surin, meet Harry and Mali. Mali and Harry, meet Surin," my Dad said to the man, who immediately knelt down and gave us an exceptionally good neck rub, which told us in no uncertain terms that he was a dedicated dawg lover. He was also our very first Khmer friend. That's what you call Cambodian Humans—but you don't say "K-merr"; you say "Ku-mare." Otherwise, no one will have a clue what you're talking about.

Flashy lights for a while, more driving, and then an enormously long lineup of vehicles at a complete standstill. It had stopped raining, so our Mom took us for a widdle and a walk to the very front of the line, where we could see water. "It won't be long now," she said, which obviously meant we were waiting for something else. It turned out to be a very rickety old boat to take us across the Mekong River. Once we got on, the cars were so jammed together, there wasn't enough room to open the door and get out, but Surin rolled down the windows so we could get a whiff of our new country. It was almost like the Sông Sài Gòn, with its *nước mắm* (fish sauce), except a little sweeter with a smoky smell drifting through it. I put it in my database under Ku-mare Scents.

Once we'd rumbled down the ramp on the other side, we kept right on going. The rain had left the sky clear, and the day was giving way to twilight. A warm glow signaled the sun was setting and it would soon be dark, and we could see silhouettes of birds swooping up and down against the colors. The road was narrow and bumpy, and we bounced from pothole to pothole, getting stuck behind cars and farmers' trucks, passing old wooden houses on stilts with animals underneath and dim yellow light flickering inside. People stood or sat on little stools all along the roadside, selling water or just watching the world go by.

Ever so slowly, the darkness became the light of a city, with cars, motorbikes and shop houses, and it wasn't long before we were on a dirt road with real houses, like An Phú, peeking out from behind high walls with loopy wires all along the top. As we drove up the street, my Dad became more and more excited. "Almost...almost...almost." And then, "We're...home!" We'd stopped in front of a yellow house with a blue-and-green gate. Surin beeped the horn, and a second later, a boy with a bright, beaming face rushed out to greet us, followed by another who looked exactly like him. After a while, we discovered

that one or the other was always with us. Their names were Soreak and Sorin, and they never stopped smiling.

Once again, our Dad had found a perfect house for us in our new city—Phnom Penh. Some Human expats call it PP for short, but our Mom and Dad don't do that, because it's the only command Mali obeys. The garden is a little bit like the one in Ho Chi Minh City, with grass, banana trees and beautiful pink bushes near the front porch, where we lie in the shade next to Sorin and Soreak's hammock. There are tiles on all sides, so you can get up to optimum speed if you do your laps all the way around the outside of the house. There's also a big porch upstairs, where we spend half our life snoozing or lying underneath the table close to our Mom and Dad.

The house has four floors, but the top one is Off Limits and kept locked 24/7—at least it's supposed to be. The only time we're allowed up there is with our Mom and Dad, and it's like being on the top of a mountain. There's always a cool breeze and you can see millions of red rooftops and the spirals of all the temples, as well as a ginormous tower, with all kinds of colorful flags, which mean it's a very important place in PP. But it's too dangerous for us, because only one side of the roof goes down to a patio and there's a sheer drop on the other side. If we were to ever go on a tear, which we've been known to do, and scramble up and over, we'd be gonzo, and I mean SPLAT! Four floors below, as in "Here marks the spot of Harry and Mali's demise.

After a zoom around the garden and dinner, our Mom and Dad took us up to our new bedroom, which we were supposed to be sharing with them, except our Dad had pretty much taken over the entire

room. His clothes were in little piles all over the floor and his scent was everywhere, which meant we weren't going to wake up in the middle of the night feeling disoriented and depressed in an empty house like I'd done before. Mali immediately splayed herself out on a pile of his underwear, just as you'd expect, and I lay on some golf shirts right beside her. It couldn't have been more than a nanosecond before we nodded off, and it must have been a good Stage 3 of our snooze cycle, because when we woke up, we were woozy and the sun was streaming in the window.

* * *

We flew down the stairs and out onto the porch, where another of those Golden opportunities was sitting on our doorstep, at least I was pretty sure that's what it was: our tennis balls, our Chuckit, some towels, a few small bags and our Science Diet, just like when Hu`ng came in his van and took us to Long Hai. The side doors and back of Surin's van were open, and when he started putting everything inside, I knew. After only one sleep in our new house in Phnom Penh, we were going on a special outing, and it was looking like the beach. As soon as I started zooming around the van, wagging and barking, Mali copied me, even though she didn't know a thing about real beaches, special out-

ings or sleepovers. WHOA! Was she going to love this! Once everything was loaded, including us, we were beach bound.

The road was smooth most of the way, and the only other vehicles were trucks like the one that was bringing our house from Ho Chi Minh City, pickups filled with Khmer Moms and Dads and children, and heavily loaded carts being pulled by enormous white cows with humps on their backs. Mali and I leaned our heads out the window and watched the scenes change from villages to coconut groves, then rolling hills. The only bumpy road we had to drive on was the steep one that went up to our hotel. In fact, you couldn't even call it a road. It was just jagged rocks and giant boulders, and we kept lurching from side to side and almost slipping off the edge! After we arrived, Surin checked the bottom of the van where we'd hit rocks for a long time.

We had to go down about a million stairs to get to our little house, but we didn't care, because we'd thunder down as fast as we could and watch all the Humans who were coming up leap to one side and plaster themselves against the railing as if it was a life-and-death situation, when it was just Mali and me on our Christmas holiday in Sihanoukville, Cambodia, December 2004.

This is inside our little house, where we regrouped and slept and had room service when our Mom and Dad went to the restaurant. It was a lot fancier than what we were used to, with white sheets on our bed and netting that Mali got her claws caught in. She pulled it down by accident when she was rolling on the bed, then shredded it beyond recognition. I heard my Mom say, "Mosquito netting isn't all that expensive" (?!!?).

When she was washing our paws the next day after a full day at the beach, she went on and on about us being "high maintenance." I think it had something to do with the paw prints on the bed. She tried to keep us off, but we couldn't really help it, seeing as it was where we were sleeping. We stayed on the porch or in the room when they went for dinner, which wasn't really a problem because we were so

exhausted from going up and down the stairs and swimming that we could barely move. We were allowed to go up to the restaurant with our Mom and Dad for breakfast a few times, and we could see the sparkle of the water from where we lay and the waves breaking in long, frothy curves.

The beach was completely different from Long Hai and Coconut Landing. Maybe all beaches are different, even though they have the same shells. There was a little bay just for us, with soft, white sand

that felt like powder between our toes and big rocks we could walk out to. The water was so clear you could see right to the bottom, even when you were standing up to your neck.

In the mornings, we'd cross over the rocks to another beach with a beautiful, long stretch of white sand that went forever, and our Mom and Dad would throw tennis balls in the water for us to fetch all the way to the end of the beach and back. After we found our balls in the surf, we'd ride the waves into shore.

Every time my Mom swam out a long way, I swam right beside her. When she first went in, I stayed on the beach barking like crazy, but in the next breath I'd charge in and swim as fast as I could to catch up to her. I don't know why, but I was worried that something might happen to her. Mali doesn't understand the concept of worrying about anything, so she never swam out.

The owner of the hotel's name was Lena. If she liked you, she'd call you "darling," and it would be "darling" this and "darling" that, but if she didn't, she could be very unfriendly. Our Mom and Dad sat and talked to her quite a bit, so we were on her good side, but some of the other guests weren't, and they didn't get pancakes in the morning. My Humans said she was married to a prince before, and maybe she was, because she told them she still goes inside the big palace. Our Mom and Dad go inside when their friends come to visit, but they'd never let dawgs in.

We stayed at the beach for quite a few sleeps, and when we got back, the whole inside of our house was white, with a new scent to add to our database. As best I could tell, it was a blend of the fumes at the gas station with a special additive that made it seem cleaner and fresher. I liked it, but my Mom said it was toxic (!??!). A wall in our house had magically moved, which meant we could charge through the living room, into the breakfast room/kitchen and out the other side on the slippery floor.

Still no sign of the big truck from our old house in An Phú, though. The morning after we got back, our Dad went to work and our Mom went someplace and waited all day. When she came home she had a fairly major meltdown, so Mali and I sat with her on the front steps to try to make her feel better, but she kept on being discouraged. I think it was the whole move catching up like they always do.

CHAPTER 15
Home in Phnom Penh

Soreak and Sorin were about the best friends you could ask for. When our Mom and Dad left the day after we got back from the beach, Sorin took us for a walk in our neighborhood, then sat with us near his hammock in the shady part of the driveway. Every once in a while, he'd get our tennis balls and throw them, then we'd chill out some more. We spent quite a bit of time exploring different parts of the house and searching out the best places for our a.m. and p.m. zzzzzzzzs, which is a critical part of the acclimation process.

Our Mom left early the next day to go and wait again, and after she came back, she had another meltdown. When my Dad got home, she went on about "the fridge and folk art"[12] (?!!?). His response was incredulous. "You've got to be kidding. What planet are we on, for Gawd's sake?"

More tears the next afternoon, until my Dad walked in. "Don't worry, honey," he said in a totally reassuring voice. "This is going to be signed off tonight," and he pulled a huge wad of money out of

---

12 The refrigerator had mistakenly been recorded on the inventory as folk art, so customs wouldn't release anything.

his pocket. It didn't even look like money, but it was riel, all right (Cambodian currency)! Luckily Mali was outside and didn't see it.

"No," my Mom cried when she saw it. "Puh-leeze—we can't!"

"Oh yes we can," my Dad said, "and we're going to. It's the only way we'll ever see our things again. And as long as we 'pay' the right person, we'll be fine. Come on. Let's go." And they left to do something she really didn't want to do. They "paid!" And trust me, it was only the beginning.

We were sound asleep when our Ho Chi Minh City house finally arrived in Phnom Penh but it sure didn't take us long to wake up. The foofaraw began with fireworks outside our gate, followed by the familiar sounds and usual suspects, our Mom and Dad among them, standing out on the road with the same glazed expressions they always get when the van comes. Mali and I had to be tied up on our long leashes in the garden, because the truck wouldn't fit in the driveway, and the gate had to be left open, but we were happy, wiggling and barking as loud as we could as all the smells of our lives wafted past. It was shortly after midnight on the first day of the new year when the movers arrived at our *house* in Phnom Penh and well after breakfast when they left our *home* the next morning. We'd officially arrived in Cambodia.

There was an old, beat-up white car sitting in the driveway that clearly belonged to someone, and when we heard "Come on, you guys, we're going for a car ride in your Mom's new car" (not exactly how I'd describe it), we were over the moon. We all piled in and our Dad drove us to **R**ucky Supermarket.

After we came home from our walk the next day, I heard him say, "Let's take Harry and Mali, honey, and blah, blah, blah (?!!?) out to your school. Then tomorrow you can go yourself." Since we arrived, she had shown absolutely no interest in her car.

A few minutes later, we were backing out of the driveway and heading down our bumpy dirt road. When we got to the end, we turned onto a paved street. From that point on, our Dad didn't stop talking, not once, nor did he notice our Mom wasn't responding to a single thing he was saying, not even with her usual nod to acknowledge she's listening.

"You'll turn here and then here until you get here. Then you'll turn here."

Her skin looked drawn, and her body language was changing by the second; in fact, when we got to the next turn at an enormously wide intersection, she was almost rigid. Traffic was coming and going from every compass point on the map, and most of the drivers appeared to be in a sort of trance as they made their way across the huge expanse of pavement—cars, trucks, vans, motorbikes, *tuk-tuks,* bicycles, push carts and "iron horses" (two-wheeled tractors hitched to old motorbikes) darting and careening in front, behind, between and around one another, all using some mysterious code that miraculously kept them from crashing into each other. And still my Dad droned on. "There's a sort of Zen to it," he was explaining. "We've always described it like that. How many times did we sit and watch a scene like this for fun in Hanoi and Ho Chi Minh City?"

No reaction from her.

"Forget right of way, honey. Forget whose turn it is, forget the direction the traffic is supposed to be moving in; in fact, forget every rule you've ever learned. None of them matter anymore. Put them right out of your mind—BUH-BYE—as if they never existed, and concentrate on one word—'fluid.' Just go with the flow." We sat there in stony silence as he waited for his chance to practice what he was preaching.

"Pick your spot," he continued, "then gradually move out and let the insanity flow around you. See those two cars not moving between all those motorbikes over there? They're waiting for their chance, and the bikes are flowing around them as if they're stones in a stream. And look now. The cars are gliding past each other as smoothly and fluidly as can be. It's almost like watching a ballet. Now, see what I'm doing," he marveled as he moved out into the chaos. "And you'll do exactly the same thing tomorrow. Ease out to the middle gradually, drift over to the left, then go straight until you see a dirt road on the left with a sign that says 'Northbridge.' After you've turned there, you'll be on the home stretch."

It was unbelievable. He was completely oblivious to the fact that her mouth was wide open, her skin was pallid and she looked as though she was going to throw up. His last set of instructions was the straw that broke the camel's back!

"I'm not f _ _ _ ing turning anywhere," she suddenly hissed. "In fact, I'm not driving on this road or any other gawd d_ _ _ road in this city. You have to be a total nutcase to think I'd drive through this f_ _ _ ing madness every morning to get to school. Zen or no Zen!"

Whoops! That didn't go over very well. But it didn't stop him. "Let's just drive out to the school anyway, honey," he said as if he was speaking to Mali and me. "We can all see it and maybe Harry and Mali can have a little run. You never know, you may change your mind."

She didn't!

Nevertheless, the "how to get to school" dilemma was resolved. Surin picks her up in the nice car and takes her to school, then comes back and picks up my Dad. We have the same quality time with him, just like always, until Surin comes back. Our Mom comes home in a school van at exactly the same time every day, so we're always at the gate to meet her.

* * *

We're not across a bridge and away from the city like we were in Ho Chi Minh City. We're smack in the middle, where you'd think it would be noisy, but it isn't, and my Dad just figured out why. We were lazing around on the upstairs verandah after dinner the other night, when his voice burst through the silence. "That's it!" he exclaimed. "No unbroken sound of horns 24/7." And he was right. Barely a sound was heard, other than what floats between moments: a few distant cries from cicadas and a soft rustle from the leaves in the banana tree moved by an invisible wind passing through it. We'd left the horns in Vietnam with the van.

We've settled into our routine, with runs in the morning either around the neighborhood or along the wide green boulevards, which my Humans say are there "because of the French," even though we haven't seen a baguette lady yet. The main boulevard has a fountain at the far end, where Mali sometimes goes swimming. After her dip, we cross onto another expanse of green, then in front of the palace where the king lives. We actually saw him driving down the street one morning in an open car like Lemon Loaf. He was standing and waving to everyone, but his hair wasn't blowing in the breeze, because he doesn't have any. Our Mom pulled back on our leashes and made us stand perfectly still to show respect. Before he became king, he was a ballet dancer in Paris.

The boulevard closest to our house is the best place in the entire city in the mornings, with all kinds of Humans and dawgs out walking and jogging, dancing with fans, jumping up and down to music and doing these long, slow stretches called tai chi with a teacher. We've never seen anyone doing tai chi before, so we always stop and watch. At first, it looked quite promising— sort of like a Khmer style of yoga— but now we're not so sure. No one does downward-facing dawg or cobra or anything that comes close to Mali's frog pose. Instead, they go

through this whole series of bizarre poses in slow motion. My Mom says it comes from China and it's supposed to make your mind and body ree-lax. Trust me, their bodies are so ree-laxed they're practically comatose. The other day, I decided to stir things up a bit by whipping around as fast as I could to see if I could catch even the teensiest bit of movement. But nothing—I'm talking NADA, not even a nose twitch or an eyelash flicker.

After the body phase, they go into a mind phase. Talk about totally "out there." This little one looks like she's off in la la land, right? Completely spaced out. Why? Because she is. She's crossed over into the same zone the drivers go to when they Zen their way through the big road near my Mom's school.

Something else we didn't see in Vietnam were zillions of monks all

decked out in bright orange robes, except it's not called orange here; it's called saffron. They're on our street almost every morning, standing outside the houses with their offerings bowls, and they don't just smile at us; they beam. They don't like wearing shoes.

Anyway, back to our day to day. There's been a huge turn of events in our lives this week. Believe it or not, our Mom has started driving! She came home from school the other day, took her things inside, called Mali and me, and we drove to **R**ucky Supermarket in her old, beat-up car. On the way home, she was so excited she went around the traffic circle at least five or nineteen times, and when I looked at her, she had this dreamy, faraway expression on her face. Now she's Zenning her way all over the city like she's been doing it forever. Stage Three of culture shock. She's "gone native."

Our Dad is very proud of her, but man, do the PO-LEECE ever see her coming. And the minute they spot us floating around a corner or drifting across a big street, they're on to us. The other day, she tried to tell them she'd never been to the corner near the bank and didn't know she couldn't turn there, and the policeman just started laughing. "I know you before," he said. "You no say that. I see you here—*same same* place, *same same* time. You know no turn." She paid and we watched him glance around quickly, then put the money in his pocket. I guess everyone gives in eventually. We drove off at a snail's pace.

CHAPTER 16
Dog on a Hot Tin Roof and a Few Surprises

Something happened today that was reminiscent of one of the unanswered questions when Mali got through the closed door in Ho Chi Minh City and decided to have her cake and eat it too! Did she open the door then, and did she open the door to the Off Limits roof garden today? And, if she didn't, who did?

Our Mom and Dad's good friend, another Mr. Gary, arrived this morning from Ho Chi Minh City to visit us for a few days. The first thing my Mom and Dad did was take him on a tour of our house, so I tagged along. Mali didn't come, and I figured she was still out in the back with Soreak, playing with her ball.

We started in the den, then moved into the living room, the breakfast room, through the kitchen and out to the laundry room, where Sifat, another of our NVBFs in Cambodia, does her magic every day. She comes in the morning, when we're having our quality time with our Dad, and stays until dinnertime. Sifat's the first magic Human I've ever met. I'm not sure how she does it, but with the flick of a switch on the washing machine, she somehow turns all the white sheets and pillowcases, the towels, my Dad's shirts and underwear, my Mom's tops, skirts, underpants and bras a beautiful color of purple. Not just

any old purple—bright purple. I bet she could be on one of those magic shows we watch on TV if she wanted. And she's adding new tricks all the time using the same switch. My Mom keeps telling my Dad, "If I wanted purple, I would have bought purple," but nothing changes. When we had guests last week, she turned everything pink.

On to the next part of the tour: the second floor, with our bedroom and the nice slippery hall in the middle, the guest room, the verandah and the office. Then the third floor, with two rooms that are never used. Finally, we were going up the last set of stairs to the roof garden. The door was slightly open, but they were talking so much they didn't notice. As soon as we stepped outside into the bright sunlight, I felt the breeze I always feel when we're on top of the world brush against my face and run through my fur. My Mom and Dad were yakking and pointing out things as they looked out over the red rooftops and spires of all the temples, and Mr. Gary was taking it all in—until he suddenly stopped dead in his tracks. "What in Gawd's name is that dog doing on the roof?" he cried out in astonishment. And there was Mali, standing absolutely frozen, three-quarters of the way down the side, with no ledge and nothing to stop her from plunging to a certain death.

In an instant, my Dad was on the roof, crawling on his hands and knees to the top. She hadn't moved a hair, but she must have sensed him coming, because when he reached the ridge, she lifted her head and locked her eyes directly into his, pleading for him to help her. I had never seen her look so fragile or so frightened. In soft, soothing tones, he repeated her name over and over, coaxing her to come to him. "It's okay, Mali, you can do it. I know you can. Come on, little one. We're going to do this one step at a time." The same gentle words Mr. Ian had used with me in Hong Kong.

Ever so slowly, she took her first tentative step, then another and another, pausing to take deep breaths as if she knew they'd stop the terror from racing through her quivering limbs. She was gradually closing the gap, and when she was an arm's length away, my Dad reached down, grabbed her collar and pulled her up over the top to safety. She scampered down onto the garden patio, across to the other side and into my Mom's outstretched arms as fast as her short little legs would carry her. There was one huge collective sigh of relief and enough neck rubs and "Good girl, Malis" to keep her going for a long time.

They were still breathing huge sighs of relief over dinner and wine later and will undoubtedly tell the story over and over. Like all Mali's stories, they can tell it exactly as it happened. It needs no embellishment. She hasn't ventured beyond the second floor since. Why and how the door was open remains a mystery.

* * *

Soreak, Sorin and Sifat are now our very, very best friends in Cambodia, because they're with us every day. They all call our Mom "Mommy," which makes her deliriously happy. I'm getting the feeling that "Mommy's" special birthday is coming up very soon, because my Dad keeps saying "Only (?!!?) more days until sixty, honey," and she replies in a teasing tone, "Oh my Gawd, I'll be as old as you are—over the hill!"

A few days ago, Max and Riley's Mom phoned from somewhere close to wish her a happy birthday. The reason I know is I heard my Mom blurt out, "Sixty, Deeds! Can you believe it? Six zee-ro. Who would have thought?" Then she asked her something about a boat. She spoke for a few more minutes and ended with, "Oh, me, too. You can't begin to imagine how much I wish this could have worked." After she hung up, she was very sad, and my Dad did his best to make her feel better.

"They tried very hard to back it up so they could come, honey," he said. "But they couldn't. Don't worry, you and I are going to have the best birthday ever, okay?"

This morning, they took us for a long walk past the fountain and down to the river, and when we got back, Surin was here with the nice car (i.e., my Dad's). I'm not sure what happened to it, but it wasn't here last night. I figured something was broken, because he was asking Surin if it was okay now. "Done," Surin said with a huge smile. I think I even saw him wink! "*Awkun nah*" (thank you), my Dad responded in his fluent Khmer, which consists of those two words.

"We've got the car back, so let's go find the blah, blah, blahs (?!!?) we need for the verandah, come back home, take Harry and Mali someplace fun, then get ready for our dinner tonight! But first, how about a good breakfast at Java?" he asked my Mom without waiting for an answer. "I'm starving!" And they left.

And guess who was sitting on the verandah at Java, casually reading the newspaper when they walked in? Max and Riley's Mom and Dad, Deeds and David, my Mom's VBFs of all time! My Dad said my Mom "nearly died when she saw them," then "burst into tears." She was so sure they weren't coming, and a little while later, there they were, driving through our gate. There was nothing wrong with the car; Surin had gone to the airport to pick them up and drop them off at Java Café, where they were waiting to give my Mom the biggest and best surprise of her entire life.

This is our album of their visit. From top left clockwise: the big surprise at Java; Mali trying to horn in when Deeds is patting me; my Mom and Dad and David standing on the big street waiting to be run over; Deeds and my Mom yakking and shopping; me hiding in the bushes at my Mom's school and all of us chilling out on the verandah.

Mali didn't even know Deeds and David, because she's never lived in Canada, but as soon as Max and Riley's Mom said, "How's my old friend, Harry?" she started worming her way in, and by the time we were inside, she was doing this irritating pawing she does when she wants someone to pat her.

For two days and one sleep, happiness floated out into our neighborhood from the upstairs verandah. It echoed through our house when my Dad and David found Deeds's missing passport in the garbage, and it skipped from the kitchen to the living room as dinner was being prepared. We took them everywhere: to the river, the *wats* (temples), my Dad's office, along the wide boulevards and out to my Mom's school. Unfortunately, we couldn't go to the palace or any live markets with them, because of the likelihood of pandemonium breaking out, based on prior incidents.

The sad part was it was over way too quickly. It seemed as though they'd just arrived and suddenly they were jumping into the car to rush to the airport. You can be sure our Dad gave them one more lasting memory of Phnom Penh as he Zenned his way through traffic, letting the insanity flow around him. Their visit was the best birthday present my Mom has ever had.

* * *

The next surprise came a few weeks later, when their other VBFs and my friend Cindy's Humans arrived from Canada. Their names are Steph and Alan, and they love dawgs more than anyone we know. Cindy and I were puppies together in Vancouver, and she's like the most Lilliputian dawg you've ever seen in your whole life, except she thinks she lives in a huge body. Cindy would take on a Rottweiler without batting an eye.

Cindy's Humans didn't just stay in Phnom Penh; they visited all kinds of places, like Angkor, which is this very old city in Cambodia that was covered over with jungle for a long time. When they came back, we did a lot of things together, like going for long walks and driving to my Mom's school or down to the river. Of course, we weren't allowed to go to the market where they buy all their Jack DVDs. They're still into it, and Mali and I are glued to the TV next to them almost every night, watching Jack yelling into his cell phone and trying to cut the wires. Sifat worked her magic on all of Cindy's

Mom's brand-new underwear right before they left, and my Mom apologized for an entire day. Sifat's doing mostly purple these days.

CHAPTER 17
A Door

It's Hotter than Hot right now and Mali and I are staying inside on the cool tiles most of the time, except in the mornings, when we go for our walks. Soreak's hammock is under the roof, and I like sleeping beside him or on the upstairs verandah with the fans whirling above. Mali wants to be wherever I am, but we can't all fit on Soreak's hammock, so she sleeps underneath when it's my area of choice.

I seem to be drinking huge amounts of water lately, which makes me pee a lot, and for the past few days, I've only eaten small bites of my food. I think it's just too hot to be hungry. Of course, my Mom and Dad were sick with worry when I didn't eat anything at all for dinner and took me to the French doctor early the next morning. He did some tests and wanted me to stay in his hospital house overnight so I could have the bottle with special water like I had in Hanoi. He took me to a kennel in the back of his house, and my Mom sat next to me while he put the tube in my leg. After it was done, she hugged me and said she'd see me right after school.

A door.

When she came back, she brought some of my favorite chicken, but I still wasn't hungry, so she curled up next to me and we lay there for a long time, feeling the warmth and comfort of each other. I could feel myself drifting off, but the second she stood up to leave, I tried to get up to go with her and pulled the tube out of my leg. She waited while the doctor put it in again, then settled me back into my kennel, promising she'd be back soon with my Dad. I don't know how long I slept, but when I woke up they were there, sitting on the floor right beside me, with their hands resting on my back, massaging it gently, speaking in quiet voices, telling me that everything was going to be all right.

Yes, a door.

All I wanted was to go home. "Just one more sleep, Hars," my Mom whispered as they were leaving. "I'll be back tomorrow to take you home." Except when she came, the doctor said I had to stay "a little longer." He may have even told her not to come the next day, or the next, because it upset me too much too see her. I don't know whether she did. I wasn't really sure of anything when I was at the French doctor's house.

Looking for a door.

But then she really was there, and I knew I was going home. I was so overjoyed, I wanted to prance up and down and bark love and gratitude, except I couldn't. All I could do was lie in the front seat of the car beside her with my head resting in her lap. When we got home, she tried to persuade me to eat, but I couldn't do that either. So I've been wandering, and my Mom goes everywhere I go.

I have to find the door.

I lie down for a while on the carpet or in the back hall, but then I need to drink some water, and I have to go out again because I know the water is going to come back up. I go around to the far side of the house and lie on the tiles, then to the back hall, and my Mom follows me. She lies down right next to me, but we only stay for a short time before I have to go someplace else.

I don't know what's happening to me…

Just now, I did something I've never done in my life, and it was that power inside me that made me do it. I walked to the gate and tried to get out. I never want to go out at night, but I stood there, barking

and whining for my Mom to please, please let me go. She spoke softly to me and brought me back inside. We've been doing this all night. I just can't stay in one place for very long.

The door is nearby; I can sense it.

It's daylight now, and I've finally settled down on the red carpet beside my Mom. Mali and my Dad are here, too. We're all huddled together, our tight little family of four. The doctor arrives. My Dad takes my head in his hands, leans so close to me that I can see nothing but his eyes, brimming with love, burrowing into me. He says my name, over and over. I sense the doctor hovering above me, and then, there, the door that I was looking for,

it's here

it's opening

it's open

I bolt through it

and instantly feel the joy and freedom of running where I've been a thousand times in my dreams with Brie, bounding across snow-covered fields, with pure white crystals lacing our tails and dotting our freezing-cold noses, a clean, icy spray spewing out behind us. And when I reach the other side and disappear into the magical forest of evergreens, the shadows are dancing joyfully on the snowy boughs, the sun is shining through their branches like I've never seen it shine before and Brie is racing toward me.

EPILOGUE
Gawdspeed Harry, by Mali Howard

When Surin came, I got into the van with my Mom and Dad and Harry. I lay like I always do, with my head on Harry's tummy, where I could still feel the warmth of him from underneath his blanket. We drove quite a long way and finally turned onto a bumpy road that ended at a big temple. The monks were waiting for us in their bright orange robes. They might even have been the same monks we see on our street every morning. WHOA! Would Harry ever like that. Surin and my Dad lifted Harry out of the van and carried him to a special spot on one side of the temple and set him down. I sat between my Mom and Dad on one side, and the monks sat all around him. My Dad said there were "twelve," which sounded like a lot of monks in the same place at the same time.

One monk whispered something to Surin, who unwrapped Harry so that everyone could see him. You only had to see him once to know he was the most beautiful Golden in the whole world. I don't think any of the monks or the children lingering nearby had ever seen a dog as big or as beautiful as Harry because their mouths gaped open the second they saw him. We all sat perfectly still, listening and watching, and after a few minutes, the monks started talking all together, except it wasn't really talking; it was more like singing. My Mom said they were "chanting for Harry."

And then they did something really amazing. They sprinkled holy water and tossed pink flowers over him. They must have known how much he loved water. I mean, one of Harry's favorite things ever was having showers. Whenever my Mom and Dad would spray us with the hose to cool us down, he would stand with his head back and his eyes closed and let the water run down his face and his neck. Afterward, he'd run around the garden in circles, wiggling and wagging and shaking himself off like crazy.

He loved flowers, too. It was Harry who taught me to eat Minh's yellow flowers in Vietnam, so when the monks blessed him with lotus petals, it was like they knew him from someplace before. Harry had about a million more scents in his database than me, so he would have caught the fragrance before the petals were even tossed and taken it with him.

While all this was going on, a monk came and spoke to Surin, who stood up and went to the van, then drove down the road we'd come in on. The monks kept on talking and singing to Harry, sprinkling the water and throwing the lotus petals, until Surin came back. Then another monk, sitting closest to the Buddha, nodded to Surin, who stepped forward and put a silver bowl down on the mat in front of Harry.

Oh My Dawg! Surin had brought an offering. It was a bowl of rice. My mouth immediately started watering, and I couldn't stop it. I knew I shouldn't be thinking about food, and I really wasn't. I was thinking about Harry and how much he loved offerings. It was Harry who said, "You have to try to ignore them, but it's pretty hard, and all you can do is your best."

Suddenly, I knew what I had to do. It was crystal clear; in fact, I don't think I've ever been so sure of anything in my life. I could see Harry with a huge smile on his face, and he was telling me to "go for it!" More than anything, he wanted me to have his offering!

I also knew I had to be the absolute best dawg I'd ever been when I went up to receive it, but I had someone to help me. I had Harry, and he guided me every step of the way. Instead of flying up to where Surin had placed the offering bowl, then chomping it down in manic mouthfuls like I usually do, I stood up, walked very slowly and calmly to the mat, lowered my head and began eating, taking time to chew each mouthful carefully and swallow before the next bite, using my best newfound manners. When I was finished, I licked the bowl politely, making sure it was perfectly clean, returned to my spot between my Mom and Dad and sat with downcast eyes, giving thanks for Harry's life.

There was a little more chanting before four Humans came with a bamboo hammock. They gently lifted Harry onto it and carried him to the place they'd prepared for him. All kinds of children appeared from the other side of the temple and skipped down to the river, bringing back scoops of earth to sprinkle over Harry, and the monks came with handfuls of lotus petals for my Mom and Dad to toss. It was like a real celebration, with everyone saying good-bye to Harry and sending him on his way. The last thing my Mom and Dad did was give him a tennis ball, his blanket, a tiny Buddha and some photos to take with him.

Harry was my best friend in the entire world. I loved him more than anything, and we were even related. Imagine that—Harry, our beauty boy from Vancouver, British Columbia, Canada, and me, Mali, from Chiangmai, Chiangmai, Thailand. It doesn't get any better than that!

A NOTE FROM HARRY'S MOM

Harry died on April 11, 2005, and traveled fittingly onward as Mali described, with blessings from the monks in their saffron robes at a *wat* east of Phnom Penh. His presence lingered for a long time: the smell of him and telltale signs—his pillows, his toys in their box in a corner of the kitchen, his kennel with a FRAGILE tag still on it, his tennis balls here and there, well chewed, well loved.

He left an enormous void in our lives. We still miss his gentle nature; his nudgings and the warm, silky feel and weight of him against us; the patting of his tail on the floor at the sound of our footsteps; his excitement when he was getting ready for a run; his patience; and the boundless enthusiasm with which he greeted us at the gate every day of his life.

He was our soul mate, the most loyal friend we could ever ask for, our travel companion, running partner and protector of Brie and Mali. His life spanned ten and a half years and five countries, and all he ever asked was to give as much love as he could and be loved in return. He was truly one of God's most beautiful creatures, born with an inherent wisdom and trust beyond his years.

Four months later, we went back to Chiangmai. The breeder didn't have any puppies, but while we were there, a beautiful Red Retriever poked his head out tentatively from around a corner. He was Mali's half brother. We fell in love with him instantly and brought him back to Phnom Penh with us. In December 2005, our tight little family of four, boarded a Thai Airways flight bound for Bangkok, where we have lived ever since. Mali and Dylan were six months apart, and have been a constant joy to us, to each other and to everyone they met.

Sadly, Dylan died in 2013 from tick fever. He was one of the sweetest, gentlest souls you could ever hope to meet and will be forever missed by his Mom and Dad and his sister, Mali. We have no doubt that he was greeted with great joy by Harry and Brie and that all three are giving as much love in their new life as they did in this one. We are convinced that when our time comes, Harry, Brie, Mali and Dylan will be at the gate to greet us, in all their Golden splendor.